Our American Century

The Digital Decade · The 90s

★

By the Editors of Time-Life Books, Alexandria, Virginia

With a Foreword by Steve Case

Contents

★

Foreword

I remember the advent of the nineties very clearly. It was a time of big ideas and events that splashed across the headlines and dominated the television news—from the end of the Cold War to the beginning of a new global era, even to the rise of grunge music. At the same time, a powerful revolution was quietly being born—the dawn of the Digital Age. And, more than almost any other development, it has shaped the decade and set the stage for the new millennium much as the Industrial Revolution did for the twentieth century—forever changing the way we live our lives.

I had a good opportunity to watch these changes take place, but even so, I am

amazed at how far—and how fast—we've come. When we launched the AOL service in 1990, PCs were still just catching on, virtually no one had heard of the Internet, and the World Wide Web hadn't been invented. By 1993, around three million people had come online. By the end of the century, that number reached nearly 200 million, worldwide. The Internet has changed our expectations; it has altered the questions we ask; it has even adjusted the way we think.

And just as democracy spread around the world in the 1990s, so has the Internet been a democratizing force—giving people the same access to a wealth of information whether they live in a well-to-do suburb, a remote rural area, or the inner city. It has helped to improve healthcare by enabling doctors to consult with specialists far from home. It has strengthened our civic life by expanding the reach of news, information, and debate. It is even forging new connections and community ties across barriers of distance, class, and culture—ties with profound and hopeful implications for the future of our planet.

Young people often tell me that they feel the most exciting phase of the Internet Age is already over. Nothing could be farther from the truth. For all we know, 50 years from now, we may look back on the '90s as the Dark Ages of the Digital Revolution. But I prefer to think of it this way: In the '90s, we built a medium that changed the way we communicate, learn, and work. And in the Internet Century, we will build a medium that changes the course of history—linking people in a new, global community . . . and leaving no one behind. As the old song goes, "You ain't seen nothing yet!"

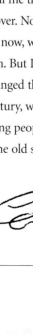

Keanu Reeves, as Neo, hero of the 1999 action–sci-fi thriller The Matrix, dodges high-tech bullets. The movie won four Academy Awards—for film editing, sound, sound effects editing, and visual effects. The special effects took two years to create.

Firefighter Chris Fields carries one-year-old Baylee Almon away from the wreckage of the Oklahoma City bombing in April 1995. The infant was pronounced dead moments later.

In what proved to be a pivotal moment in his trial, O. J. Simpson demonstrates the ill fit of the infamous bloody gloves, the left one found at the scene of the Nicole Brown Simpson and Ron Goldman murders, and the right one behind his residence in Brentwood

Four days of rain in March 1998 cause the Beaver Dam Creek to overflow its banks, flooding Elba, Alabama, and forcing the evacuation of half the town's 4,011 residents. Weather-related calamities around the globe in 1998 caused $89 billion in economic losses, 32,000 deaths, and over 300 million people to be displaced—an annual record and a threefold increase over 1997.

Lance Armstrong, 27, cycles past sunflowers to victory in the 1999 Tour de France, the world's premier bike race. His win amazed the world. Following treatment in 1997 for near-fatal testicular cancer, Armstrong resumed a rigorous training regimen— "This guy won't quit," said Karl Haussmann, director of Armstrong's self-named cancer foundation.

A 1999 photograph from the Hubble Space Telescope shows two spiral galaxies passing each other "like majestic ships in the night," as NASA put it. The 12.5-ton, school-bus-sized Hubble, with its 619-pound Wide-Field/Planetary Camera 2 system, was placed in orbit in April 1990.

Triumphs and Travails: 1990-1999

As if in preparation for the new millennium, established political, economic, scientific, and social paradigms shifted in the 1990s. Biotechnology put genetically engineered crops on the table; gene therapy promised to cure deadly diseases; and with the successful cloning of a sheep in 1996, the cloning of human beings became a distinct possibility. The global computer grid known as the Internet incited the information revolution, which exploded established boundaries, changing the way people lived, worked, communicated, and shopped. For the breadth of change it ushered in, the decade could be compared with the Industrial Revolution or the mid-1400s, when Gutenberg introduced movable type and transformed the printing process.

But optimism was not the decade's keynote—at least not in the beginning. As the '90s got under way, the country's finances were in trouble. Years of military buildup and heavy deficit spending had caused a recession and forced President George Bush to renege on his campaign promise of "no new taxes." As corporate America experienced a series of mergers, acquisitions, and restructurings, large corporations laid off employees by the tens of thousands. In 1991 American firms cut an average of more than 2,400 jobs every business day, while automobile manufacturing's Big Three—Chrysler, Ford, and General Motors—posted losses of nearly $7.5 billion. Where employees once found compensation that outpaced inflation, they now faced slashed payrolls and shrinking benefits.

But as job security became increasingly rare at home, there was good news abroad. America's archrival, the Soviet Union, was collapsing under the weight of its own political and economic troubles. Two years after the Berlin Wall fell, in 1989, Communism lost one of its most powerful forces when President Mikhail Gorbachev dissolved the Soviet Union.

A Mixed Situation. Financial ills under a Republican president failed to provide leading Democrats like Bill Bradley and Richard Gephardt with an impetus to run against George Bush. His handling of the Gulf War in 1990 had earned him a 91 percent approval rating—the highest ever for a president. Still, Bush's triumphant move in the Persian Gulf—leading an interna-

A Timeline of the '90s

1990

Nelson Mandela, *South Africa's antiapartheid movement leader, is freed after being imprisoned for more than 27 years for his political beliefs.*

The U.S. Fish and Wildlife Service *adds the northern spotted owl to the threatened-species list, igniting a controversy between environmentalists dedicated to protecting the species and loggers dependent on the timber of old-growth forests where the owls build their nests.*

Tennis star Martina Navratilova *wins her ninth Wimbledon singles title, besting Helen Wills Moody's record of eight.*

President George Bush deploys *thousands of U.S. troops and weapons to Saudi Arabia in Operation Desert Shield, a response to an invasion of oil-rich Kuwait by Saddam Hussein's Iraqi forces.*

The FDA approves Norplant, *an implant of six slim rods providing five years of birth control—the first new birth-control method since the introduction of the Pill in the mid-1960s.*

New on TV: *Seinfeld; Beverly Hills 90210; America's Funniest Home Videos; Northern Exposure; Wings; The Fresh Prince of Bel-Air; Twin Peaks; Law & Order; In Living Color.*

New products: *Teenage Mutant Ninja Turtles; Terra Chips; Gillette Sensor razor; Nantucket Nectars.*

New in print: *Scott Turow's The Burden of Proof; Larry McMurtry's Buffalo Girls; Entertainment Weekly magazine.*

The Academy Awards: *best picture—Dances with Wolves; best actor—Jeremy Irons, for Reversal of Fortune; best actress—Kathy Bates, for Misery.*

1991

Operation Desert Storm, *a combined air and ground assault on Iraqi forces in Kuwait involving 500,000 international troops, begins, ending 100 hours later with the defeat of Iraqi forces.*

In Los Angeles, Rodney King, *a 25-year-old unarmed black motorist, is severely beaten by police officers; a bystander videotapes the beating and the officers are indicted.*

William Kennedy Smith, *nephew of Senator Edward Kennedy, is accused of raping a woman at the Kennedy family estate in Palm Beach, but in the televised trial, a Florida jury finds him not guilty.*

Mount Pinatubo erupts in the Philippines, *raining ash 23 feet deep on the island of Luzon in one of the largest volcanic eruptions of the century.*

Police arrest Jeffrey Dahmer *in Milwaukee and charge him with killing 15 young men and boys when they find human skulls, heads, and other body parts in his apartment.*

Track athlete Mike Powell *leaps an incredible 29 feet 4 inches at the World Track and Field Championships, breaking Bob Beamon's 23-year-old long-jump record.*

Seventy-four years of Communist rule ends *in Russia when a Communist coup attempt fails and President Gorbachev suspends the Communist Party.*

Anita Hill, *law professor at the University of Oklahoma, charges that Supreme Court nominee Clarence Thomas sexually harassed her while they were colleagues in the '80s. Despite the charges, the Senate votes 52 to 48 to confirm Thomas as a Supreme Court justice.*

Los Angeles Lakers star Earvin "Magic" Johnson, *32, announces that he has the virus that causes AIDS and will retire immediately from basketball.*

The World Wide Web, *used by researchers to exchange information and messages, is invented by British scientist Tim Berners-Lee.*

New on TV: *Home Improvement; Herman's Head; Homefront; I'll Fly Away; The Commish.*

New products: *McDonald's McLean low-fat hamburger; Robitussin cough drops.*

tional coalition to save tiny, oil-rich Kuwait from Iraq's Saddam Hussein—could not detract attention from America's economic backslide. So when the 1992 presidential campaigns began, voters faced a mixed situation—a well-liked, foreign affairs–savvy incumbent presiding over a $4 trillion national debt and an eight-year high in unemployment (nearly 10 million Americans were out of work in mid-1992). Bush would not be reelected, but the new president—five-term Arkansas governor William Jefferson Clinton—would not, in the eyes of the voting public, be a clear-cut winner either: He eked out the presidency with just 43 percent of the popular vote.

Clinton fashioned himself as a progressive leader. He had promised that the ethnic and gender makeup of his White House would resemble that of the nation at large, and he decried politicians who wrote bad checks against the House bank and ate free lunches at the House restaurant. When speaking about emotional issues—such as homosexuals in the military or the struggles of working- and middle-class families, who had failed to benefit from the economic boom of the 1980s—he became emotional himself, displaying sympathy and resolve. He voiced concern about the country's children and the Generation Xers, who faced a job market in which only minimum-wage positions in the fast-food industry were on the rise. He worried that the Social Security coffers would soon be empty. His youth, love of fast food, and ability to name the price of a loaf of bread made him seem more in touch with the average American than his predecessors.

But at times it was hard to discern whether Bill Clinton was a Democrat or a Republican. He espoused free trade, welfare reform, and fiscal conservatism, but also believed in universal healthcare, giving the working poor a leg up, and a woman's right to choose abortion. A versatile politician whose boundless empathy soothed the nation in times of disaster, Bill Clinton often failed to take decisive action in the face of political risk. During his eight years in the White House, he simultaneously reinvented the Democratic Party and besmirched the office of the president.

Once in office, Clinton wavered on issues he previously felt strongly about, from gays in the military to how to handle a clutch of refugees from Haiti. His credibility was questioned as his involvement in a dubious real-estate development company called Whitewater came to light, and his ambitious healthcare-reform package, spearheaded by First Lady Hillary Rodham Clinton, was buried in the fallout of the Whitewater imbroglio. Then Clinton became the first Democrat since Harry Truman to lose control of the House when Republicans

New in print: *Whitney Otto's How to Make an American Quilt; Josephine Hart's Damage; Amy Tan's The Kitchen God's Wife.*

The Academy Awards: *best picture—The Silence of the Lambs; best actor—Anthony Hopkins, for The Silence of the Lambs; best actress—Jodie Foster, for The Silence of the Lambs.*

1992

New York Mafia boss John Gotti *is convicted of murder, extortion, and obstruction of justice and is sentenced to life in prison without parole.*

Riots break out in South Central Los Angeles, *resulting in the deaths of more than 50 people and more than $1 billion worth of property damage, after a California jury acquits the L.A. policemen involved in the 1991 beating of Rodney King.*

Hurricane Andrew *hits Florida south of Miami, killing 30 people and causing $20 billion worth of damage, before moving on to devastate areas of Louisiana.*

Bill Clinton and Al Gore *are elected president and vice president, defeating Republican incumbents George Bush and Dan Quayle as well as Reform Party candidates Ross Perot and Admiral James Stockdale.*

A U.S.-led military intervention, *sanctioned by the UN Security Council, arrives in Somalia, where famine has killed 300,000 people and the nation is falling into anarchy.*

New on TV: *Melrose Place; Jerry Springer; Love and War; Mad About You; Picket Fences; Martin.*

New products: *Dodge Viper; Chicken Tonight; nicotine patches.*

New in print: *Robert James Waller's The Bridges of Madison County; Cormac McCarthy's All the Pretty Horses; John Gray's Men Are from Mars, Women Are from Venus; Dorothy Allison's Bastard Out of Carolina; Rush Limbaugh's The Way Things Ought to Be.*

The Academy Awards: *best picture—Unforgiven; best actor—Al Pacino, for Scent of a Woman; best actress—Emma Thompson, for Howards End.*

1993

Beginning a scandal dubbed "Nannygate," Zoë Baird, *President Clinton's attorney general-designate, apologizes for employing two undocumented immigrants for household help and for neglecting to pay Social Security taxes on their salaries, then becomes the first U.S. cabinet nominee in 120 years to withdraw from consideration.*

A van loaded with explosives, *allegedly planted by Muslim fundamentalists, explodes in the parking garage under New York's World Trade Center, killing six and injuring more than a thousand.*

After a 51-day standoff at the Branch Davidian compound in Waco, Texas, *FBI assault vehicles pump tear gas into the fortress and hours later the building goes up in smoke. More than 80 people, including the group's leader, 34-year-old David Koresh, died.*

Lorena Bobbitt, 24, of Manassas, Virginia, *cuts off her husband John's penis with a kitchen knife in retaliation for years of alleged abuse and forced sex.*

Two-year-old Baby Jessica *is returned to her biological parents, Dan and Cara Schmidt, after a two-year legal battle between the Schmidts and Jan and Roberta DeBoer, who had been in the process of adopting the child when the Schmidts decided they wanted their daughter back.*

Several months after the tragic murder of his father, basketball star Michael Jordan *announces that he will retire from basketball, explaining that it holds no more challenges for him.*

Jurassic Park, *directed by Steven Spielberg, becomes the highest-grossing movie of all time when it makes $712 million in ticket sales worldwide.*

swept the 1994 midterm elections. As Republican congressman Newt Gingrich shepherded his "Contract with America" agenda through the House, Clinton seemed doomed. However, when Gingrich, as Speaker of the House, angered Americans by forcing a government shutdown over a budget dispute, Clinton bounded back into action and deftly coopted Republican issues such as crime, welfare reform, and a balanced budget. With interest rates down, jobs on the rise, and a recovering economy on his side, Clinton kept a firm hold on the presidency, easily defeating Kansas senator Bob Dole in the '96 election.

"Building a Bridge to the 21st Century." Clinton's campaign promise to build "a bridge to the 21st century" coincided perfectly with the appearance of the World Wide Web—a sort of electronic filing cabinet in which computer users could connect to other computers and retrieve documents by typing in key words. Invented by British software developer Tim Berners-Lee, the Web was spun out to the public in 1991, unleashing an economic force that, together with the economy-stimulating legislation Bill Clinton pushed through Congress, helped turn the country's economic tide. By 1999, 80 million Americans used personal computers to pay their bills, e-mail family and friends, and surf the Internet, and this widespread use of technology helped fuel the longest bull market in financial history.

While the stock market of the 1980s, which was bullish on mergers, acquisitions, and junk bonds, had belonged to a select few, the market of the mid- to late-'90s—spurred by the price of stocks in Internet start-up and other high-tech companies—seemed to belong to everyone. It was the widest democratization of the market since the 1920s. Corporate America took on a distinctly dressed-down look, a reflection of the young entrepreneurs who chaired the hottest companies listed on the high-tech dominated NASDAQ exchange. Writers, plumbers, and schoolteachers liquidated life-insurance policies and bonds to buy stock in "dot-com" companies (so called because commercial Web-site "addresses" included a period, "dot," followed by the three-letter domain name "com"). Some Americans traded stocks directly from their homes through online services. Eighties prosperity and big spending were reborn. Federal Reserve chairman Alan Greenspan kept interest rates in check, and more people than ever bought homes that, like the sport utility vehicles parked in front of them, were built bigger and bigger. The income gap between the rich and the poor, despite Clinton's best intentions, also grew. For the first time since perhaps Andrew Carnegie, America was home to the world's richest individual: software

Writer Toni Morrison, *author of six novels, including Beloved, becomes the first African-American woman to receive the Nobel Prize in literature.*

Dr. Jack Kevorkian, *nicknamed "Dr. Death," participates in his 19th assisted suicide and is imprisoned for violating Michigan's law against such practices.*

Congress passes the Brady Bill, *named for former press secretary James Brady, which requires a waiting period of up to five days for the purchase of handguns.*

The North American Free Trade Agreement (NAFTA), *which will phase out all tariffs and other trade barriers between the U.S., Canada, and Mexico over a 14-year period, is signed into law by President Clinton.*

Sixty-nine percent of Americans say they believe in angels, *according to a Time/CNN poll.*

New on TV: *The X-Files; Frasier; Dr. Quinn, Medicine Woman; NYPD Blue; Grace Under Fire; Dave's World; Diagnosis Murder; The Nanny; Homicide.*

New products: *Beanie Babies; Scotch-Brite Never Rust Wool Soap Pads; Pentium processor.*

New in print: *E. Annie Proulx's The Shipping News; William J. Bennett's The Book of Virtues; Wally Lamb's She's Come Undone; John Grisham's The Client.*

The Academy Awards: *best picture—Schindler's List; best actor—Tom Hanks, for Philadelphia; best actress—Holly Hunter, for The Piano.*

1994

U.S. figure skater Nancy Kerrigan, *after finishing a practice session in Detroit, Michigan, is clubbed on the knee, an attack planned by associates of Tonya Harding, Kerrigan's top competitor for the U.S. national figure skating title.*

The trials of brothers Erik and Lyle Menendez, *accused of murdering their parents in order to inherit their $14 million estate, are both declared mistrials when juries are unable to reach verdicts.*

American speed skater Bonnie Blair *wins two gold medals at the Winter Olympics in Lillehammer, Norway, bringing her career total to five, the most gold medals of any American female athlete. In the most watched event, Ukrainian Oksana Baiul wins the gold medal for figure skating, while Nancy Kerrigan wins the silver.*

An early-morning earthquake *registering 6.7 on the Richter scale rocks Los Angeles, collapsing buildings and freeways, killing 61 people, and causing more than $20 billion in damage.*

Kurt Cobain, *lead singer of the influential rock band Nirvana, dies of a self-inflicted gunshot wound at age 27.*

Former president Richard Nixon, *81, the only U.S. president in history to resign from office, suffers a stroke at his home in Park Ridge, New Jersey, and dies a few days later.*

Paula Jones, *a former Arkansas state employee, accuses President Bill Clinton of sexually harassing her in a hotel room in 1991, when he was governor of Arkansas, and files suit against him for $700,000 and a public apology.*

Jacqueline Kennedy Onassis, *widow of President John F. Kennedy, succumbs to cancer at age 64 and is buried next to her first husband, in Arlington National Cemetery.*

After leading Los Angeles police on a 90-minute chase in his Ford Bronco, *an event televised around the world, O. J. Simpson is arrested for the murders of his ex-wife Nicole Brown Simpson and her friend Ronald Goldman.*

In Union, South Carolina, Susan Smith *claims her two children, ages three years and 14 months, were kidnapped during a carjacking, but later admits that she murdered the children herself.*

tycoon Bill Gates of Redmond, Washington. Gates's behemoth software company, Microsoft, utterly—and unfairly, according to the Justice Department—dominated the market. The government filed an antitrust suit against Gates in 1999, and in 2000 mandated that his company be split in half.

Going Global. The most powerful force behind the information revolution was e-commerce, a largely unanticipated offshoot of the Web. The selling of goods and services on the Internet rapidly transformed the network into a global marketplace in which geography was irrelevant. During the 1998 holiday season, consumers purchased more than $8 billion worth of goods from Internet vendors. Traditional retailers scampered to establish outposts on the Web. By 1999 business-to-business e-commerce totaled more than $100 billion. As journalist Thomas Friedman wrote, computer-driven globalization took on a distinctly American face, one that "wears Mickey Mouse ears, . . . eats Big Macs, . . . drinks Coke or Pepsi and . . . does its computing on an IBM or Apple laptop, using Windows '98, with an Intel Pentium II processor and a network link from Cisco Systems." No small number of Europeans groused about the Americanization of the planet; meanwhile, less developed countries, like Vietnam and China, eagerly opened their cyber borders to e-commerce.

There was trouble, though, in the post–Cold War Soviet Union and in Yugoslavia. Populist Boris Yeltsin emerged as the Soviet Union's new democratic leader, and nine of the country's 15 republics declared independence, throwing the region dangerously out of balance. Russia degenerated into a free-for-all nation in which organized crime joined forces with corrupt government officials, and poverty and crime ran rampant. Warring ethnic factions in Yugoslavia visited horrendous devastation on a nation that had previously enjoyed the highest standard of living in Eastern Europe. The unrest harked back eerily to the outbreak of World War I. United Nations peacekeepers failed to stop the slaughter, and reports of mass torture, rape, and genocide came to light.

In Africa, anarchy and famine consumed Somalia. There was jubilation around the world, though, when South Africa's blacks won the right to vote in 1994, officially ending 46 years of apartheid. Nelson Mandela, who had been released from prison only four years earlier, was elected the country's president. Other historic acts of progress and peace—such as the 1993 agreement between Yitzhak Rabin and Yasir Arafat, and the 1998 Good Friday accord between Great Britain, Ireland, and the Irish Republican Army, both brokered by President Clinton—provided windows of hope.

For the first time in 90 years, *there is no World Series because major-league baseball players are on strike; the dispute with the owners primarily revolves around the imposition of overall team salary caps.*

New on TV: *Friends; ER; Ellen; Party of Five; Chicago Hope; Touched by an Angel.*

New products: *the Wonderbra; Netscape Navigator; Fruitopia beverages.*

New in print: *John Berendt's Midnight in the Garden of Good and Evil; Ursula Hegi's Stones from the River; James Redfield's Celestine Prophecy; David Guterson's Snow Falling on Cedars.*

The Academy Awards: *best picture—Forrest Gump; best actor—Tom Hanks, for Forrest Gump; best actress—Jessica Lange, for Blue Sky.*

1995

For the first time in 40 years, *the Republican Party has the majority in both the House and the Senate.*

Basketball superstar Michael Jordan *announces he will come out of retirement and return to play for the NBA's Chicago Bulls.*

Shannon Faulkner *is the first woman admitted into the cadet corps of the Citadel in South Carolina but leaves, along with 35 male classmates, during the first week of infamously harsh training.*

A bomb explodes outside the Alfred P. Murrah Federal Building in Oklahoma City, *killing 169 people, including 19 young children, and injuring 614 others, while causing $500 million worth of damage.*

Cal Ripken Jr., shortstop for the Baltimore Orioles, *breaks the longstanding record of 2,130 consecutive games set by Lou Gehrig in 1939. He will go on for a total of 2,632 consecutive games before choosing not to play on September 20, 1998.*

Israeli prime minister Yitzhak Rabin is assassinated *by an Israeli law student at a peace rally in Tel Aviv's main square.*

O. J. Simpson is found not guilty *of the brutal murders of his ex-wife Nicole Brown Simpson and her friend Ronald Goldman, ending a controversial televised trial that captivated and aggravated the nation.*

New on TV: *Caroline in the City; The Single Guy; The Drew Carey Show; NewsRadio.*

New products: *BMW's Z3; blue M&Ms; Pepcid; over-the-counter Tagamet; Java programming language; Windows '95.*

New in print: *Mary Karr's The Liars' Club; Ellen Fein and Sherrie Schneider's The Rules.*

The Academy Awards: *best picture—Braveheart; best actor—Nicolas Cage, for Leaving Las Vegas; best actress—Susan Sarandon, for Dead Man Walking.*

1996

Unabomber suspect Ted Kaczynski *is arrested by FBI agents in Lincoln, Montana, and is charged with killing three people and wounding 23 others with bombs he sent through the mail over an 18-year period.*

TWA Flight 800, bound for Paris, explodes *over Long Island and plunges into the Atlantic, killing all 230 people aboard.*

A pipe bomb explodes *at the Centennial Olympic Park in Atlanta during the Summer Olympic Games, killing one person and injuring 111 others.*

Olympian Kerri Strug *seals the gold medal for the American women's gymnastics team in Atlanta after a memorable vault in which she held her landing despite an injured ankle; Michael Johnson wins two golds and sprints to the world record in the 200 meters.*

Violence at Home. America's long-held notions of safety and peace at home, however, were tested time and again. A nearly decade-long drop in crime rates nationwide made the streets feel safer, but post offices, office buildings, commuter trains, and schools felt considerably more dangerous.

On April 19, 1995, a car bomb eviscerated a federal office building in Oklahoma City, killing 169 people, including 19 children, and wounding 614. Suspicions immediately settled on Islamic terrorists, a faction of which had tried to blow up New York's World Trade Center in 1993; they killed six and injured more than 1,000. But the terrorist behind the Oklahoma attack turned out to be an American—Timothy McVeigh, a disgruntled Gulf War veteran who was angry at the government. In eight separate incidents in schools from Mississippi to Oregon, assassins as young as 11 gunned down classmates. The most chilling assault, carried out by two heavily armed students at Columbine High School in Littleton, Colorado, claimed 15 lives.

Americans were drawn together by these tragedies, but were bitterly divided by others. Violence took on racial overtones in the beating of African-American Rodney King by four white Los Angeles police officers who had arrested King after a high-speed automobile chase. Despite videotaped footage of the beating, a mainly white suburban jury acquitted the officers. Rioting erupted in South Central Los Angeles as a result. More than 50 people died, and three days of arson, looting, and vandalism touched off waves of fear and anger across the country.

But it was the most sensationalized crime of the decade—in which African-American football legend O. J. Simpson was charged with brutally killing his former wife Nicole Brown Simpson and her friend Ronald Goldman, who were both white—that starkly illustrated the chasm separating the two races. For months in 1995 the murder trial received nonstop coverage. Despite ample evidence against him, the jury, whose 12 members included nine blacks, acquitted Simpson. According to a CBS News survey, 78 percent of blacks thought that he was innocent, and 75 percent of whites that he was guilty.

The Public's Right to Know? The Simpson trial also illustrated a change in the media's relationship to the events it covered. By mid-decade it became increasingly difficult to tell whether the media was covering an event or using an event to stay in the public eye. In many cases, media coverage was driven by quantity—more airtime, more interviews, more special reports—rather than quality, and in the process Americans saw good taste, considerateness, and respect fall by the wayside.

Prince Charles and Princess Diana divorce, *ending their troubled 15-year marriage.*

For the first time since 1964, *a Democratic president is reelected for a second term and President Bill Clinton and Vice President Al Gore remain in the White House for four more years.*

President Clinton names Madeleine Albright secretary of state, *succeeding Warren Christopher and making her the first woman to hold that position in the history of the United States.*

John and Patsy Ramsey's home *in Boulder, Colorado, becomes a murder scene when their six-year-old daughter, child beauty pageant star JonBenet, is found murdered in the basement after her parents report her missing.*

New on TV: *Suddenly Susan; Spin City; The Rosie O'Donnell Show.*

New products: *Tickle Me Elmo; McDonald's Arch Deluxe hamburger; Palm Pilot; Starbuck's Frappuccino.*

New in print: *Hillary Clinton's It Takes a Village; Frank McCourt's Angela's Ashes; Sapphire's Push.*

The Academy Awards: *best picture—The English Patient; best actor—Geoffrey Rush, for Shine; best actress—Frances McDormand, for Fargo.*

1997

The Hale-Bopp comet, *bright enough to be visible to the naked eye, swings past the sun at close to 100,000 miles per hour for the first time in 4,200 years.*

Dolly, a sheep created from the cells *of an adult sheep, is introduced by researchers at the Roslin Institute in Edinburgh, Scotland. It is the first cloned mammal.*

Twenty-one-year-old Tiger Woods *wins the Masters Tournament by a record 12 strokes to become the youngest Masters champion and the first African-American to win any of the four major professional tournaments.*

Actress Ellen DeGeneres *comes out in real life and as her character on the sitcom Ellen, becoming the first openly gay lead character on a network television series.*

Timothy McVeigh, *a U.S. Army veteran with antigovernment beliefs, is convicted and sentenced to death for the 1995 bombing of a federal building in Oklahoma City. The other defendant, Terry Nichols, is found guilty of one count of conspiracy to use a weapon of destruction and eight counts of involuntary manslaughter of federal agents.*

NASA's spacecraft *Pathfinder lands on Mars and deploys a small roving vehicle, Sojourner, that analyzes the planet's geology, climate, and atmosphere while taking photographs that show the planet's terrain in unprecedented detail.*

Thirty-six-year-old Diana, *Princess of Wales, is killed in a car accident in Paris along with her beau, Dodi al-Fayed, and the driver of the car.*

Mother Teresa, *the Roman Catholic nun who won the Nobel Peace Prize for her work on behalf of the poor and sick in India, dies in Calcutta at age 87.*

New on TV: *South Park; King of the Hill; Veronica's Closet.*

New products: *V-chip; digital cameras; DVD players; Tamagotchi toys.*

New in print: *Charles Frazier's Cold Mountain; John Grisham's The Partner; Jon Krakauer's Into Thin Air; Sebastian Junger's The Perfect Storm; Arthur S. Golden's Memoirs of a Geisha.*

The Academy Awards: *best picture—Titanic; best actor—Jack Nicholson, for As Good As It Gets; best actress—Helen Hunt, for As Good As It Gets.*

The 1991 Senate confirmation hearings of Clarence Thomas, a conservative federal judge nominated to the Supreme Court by George Bush, brought one of the earliest indications that media standards were shifting. Thomas was accused of sexually harassing a former assistant, Anita Hill, when they both worked at the Department of Education and the Equal Employment Opportunity Commission. Live broadcasts and nationwide front-page attention urged the public to tune in as elected officials grappled—absurdly at times—with sexually explicit testimony. Although Thomas was ultimately confirmed and Hill was generally considered to have been wronged, the hearings—which Thomas called a "high-tech lynching"—opened the door for sexual-harassment claims.

The media devoted even more ink and footage to sexual terminology during special prosecutor Kenneth Starr's expanded Whitewater investigation, which led him to Bill Clinton's dalliance with 21-year-old White House intern Monica Lewinsky. Clinton will forever be associated with a period of global transformation and economic prosperity at home, but because the Whitewater investigation ultimately proved that Clinton himself was not up to his pledged "higher moral standard in government," he will also be linked with unseemliness and scandal. Simultaneously disgusted and intrigued, Americans were riveted by the details of the special investigation, and the media, making coverage of the revelations a 24-hour assignment, left nothing to the imagination.

The president made matters worse when he tried to explain his way out of his initial claim—made on television to the entire nation—that he had not had sexual relations with "that woman." Lewinsky's private journals, recorded phone conversations, and unsent e-mails, which had been scrutinized for savory tidbits, said otherwise. Clearly Clinton had lied, but were his indiscretions and falsehoods grounds for impeachment? By a narrow, partisan margin, the House decided they were. Clinton ultimately escaped removal from office, but when Starr's 452-page report (published in newspapers and available on the Internet) divulged the embarrassing details of his affair with Lewinsky, the office of the presidency was brought to one of its lowest points in history. Yet it may have been one public airing of private laundry too many, because when Clinton appeared on national television to apologize to his wife and the country for his indiscretions, his ratings, remarkably, climbed. Americans appeared to feel sorry for Clinton. With no help from an overzealous media, he survived.

1998

At the Winter Olympics in Nagano, Japan, *15-year-old figure skater Tara Lipinski becomes the youngest person ever to win the gold medal in figure skating.*

In Jonesboro, Arkansas, *two boys, ages 11 and 13, kill four schoolgirls and one teacher outside their middle school during a false fire alarm.*

Seinfeld, NBC's popular sitcom about the lives of four neurotic New Yorkers, airs its last episode, which is watched by an estimated 76 million people.

In a television address to the nation, *President Bill Clinton admits to having had an inappropriate relationship with former White House intern Monica Lewinsky.*

Baseball players Mark McGwire and Sammy Sosa *break Roger Maris's 1961 record of 61 home runs in a single season when they slam 70 and 66 homers, respectively.*

Seventy-seven-year-old senator John Glenn, *who in 1962 became the first U.S. astronaut to orbit the earth, returns to space aboard the space shuttle Discovery to participate in experiments about how space travel affects older people.*

Hurricane Mitch devastates Central America *with eight days of rain and 180-mile-per-hour winds that cause massive mudslides, killing 10,000 in one of the deadliest Atlantic storms in 200 years.*

Former professional wrestler Jesse *"the Body" Ventura is elected governor of Minnesota.*

New on TV: *Felicity; The Hughleys; That '70s Show; Charmed; Sports Night.*

New products: *Viagra; Volkswagen's New Beetle; Apple's iMac.*

New in print: *Tom Brokaw's The Greatest Generation; Michael Jordan's For the Love of the Game.*

The Academy Awards: *best picture—Shakespeare in Love; best actor—Roberto Benigni, for Life Is Beautiful; best actress—Gwyneth Paltrow, for Shakespeare in Love.*

1999

President Bill Clinton *is acquitted by the Senate in his impeachment trial on charges of perjury and obstruction of justice in his effort to hide sexual indiscretions with former White House intern Monica Lewinsky.*

Hockey's "Great One," Wayne Gretzky, *retires, ending an incredible 21-year professional hockey career that included 10 scoring titles, four championships, and nine MVP awards.*

At Columbine High School in Littleton, Colorado, *two armed students lay siege to the school, killing 12 students and one teacher and wounding 23 others before taking their own lives in one of the most tragic school shootings in history.*

After 78 days of air strikes by NATO forces, *Yugoslavian president Slobodan Milosevic surrenders and agrees to withdraw his troops from Kosovo.*

The U.S. women's soccer team wins *the World Cup championship when, after two scoreless overtime periods, Brandi Chastain fires the winning penalty kick past China's goalie.*

John F. Kennedy Jr., his wife, Carolyn, and his sister-in-law Lauren Bessette *are killed when the private plane Kennedy is piloting crashes into the ocean off the coast of Martha's Vineyard.*

American cyclist Lance Armstrong *wins the 2,287-mile Tour de France less than two years after battling testicular cancer.*

Turkey is hit by one of the century's worst earthquakes, *registering 7.4 on the Richter scale and killing up to 17,000 people.*

New on TV: *The PJs; The West Wing; Once and Again; Law & Order: Special Victims Unit.*

New products: *Apple's iBook; Tilex Fresh Shower.*

New in print: *Thomas Harris's Hannibal; Barbara Kingsolver's The Poisonwood Bible; Mitch Albom's Tuesdays with Morrie.*

The Academy Awards: *best picture—American Beauty; best actor—Kevin Spacey, for American Beauty; best actress—Hilary Swank, for Boys Don't Cry.*

Stars and
Icons

★

While many people stood out in their respective fields during the 1990s, some did so in remarkable ways. Whether it was in business, government, sports, or entertainment, a select few became icons of the American spirit.

Few displayed entrepreneurial leadership more boldly and successfully, if controversially, than Bill Gates. Born in 1955, Gates began programming computers at the age of 13. At age 20, in 1975, he dropped out of Harvard to start Microsoft with friend Paul Allen. In 1990, Microsoft released user-friendly Windows 3.0 for personal computers, and Gates was lauded as a hero. He had come to embody the spirit of a computer revolution in which nerdy garage and basement entrepreneurs got revenge as corporate chieftains.

But in 1997, when Microsoft attempted to capitalize on the burgeoning Web-browser market by integrating its Internet Explorer into Windows 98, Gates was vilified as the Satan of Software. The Justice Department and 20 states slapped him with an antitrust suit—he had "placed an oppressive thumb on the scale of corporate fortunes," a federal district court judge said.

In a move that made his more than $77 billion net worth appear less excessive, Gates and his wife, Melinda, endowed a foundation with more than $17 billion to combat preventable diseases, improve education, and beautify the Pacific Northwest.

Bill Gates (right) remains dedicated to technology: "Software is changing the world, and throughout my life that will continue. That's my life's work." He also supported research in biotechnology and telecommunications.

The Reluctant Warrior

"As a soldier for 35 years, it was my job to prepare young people for battle and to make sure that when they went up that hill to face an enemy, they had the skills they needed to survive."

"We are not committing mercenaries, we are committing sons and daughters."

"First we're going to cut it off. Then, we're going to kill it."—On the Iraqi army, 1991

"Presidents and [defense] secretaries don't have military problems. They have political problems, and often there is a military component. I've always tried to give them the very best component solutions to their political problems."

"I was born in Harlem, raised in the South Bronx, went to public high school, got out of public college, went into the Army, and then I just stuck with it."

"Soldiering is about people in the same value system, the same cultural system. You go from one Army post to another, you might as well have been at the last one. You immediately fit in."

"Active duty military officers have no business talking about partisan political matters. There is total confusion as to what my political philosophy might or might not be. This is the way it should be . . . it's part of our code."

"The Army has officially advised me that, for record purposes, I have served 35 years, 3 months, 21 days, and, as we say in the infantry, a wake-up. I loved every single day of it. And it's hard to leave."

"I've made myself very accessible to the black press and I do that as a way of just showing people, 'Hey, look at that dude. He came out of the South Bronx. If he got out, why can't I?' "

"I didn't expect race to be a major theme, but it kept coming up through the whole book."
—On his memoir

"I try to be the same person I was yesterday."

By the end of the Gulf War four-star general Colin Powell—the youngest chairman ever appointed to the Joint Chiefs of Staff and the highest-ranking African-American military officer in U.S. history—was a bona fide American hero. Decisive, intelligent, prudent, and media savvy, Powell personified the new post-Cold War U.S. Army. So when the veteran of two Vietnam tours—the "Reluctant Warrior," as he once called himself for his deliberate hesitation to use force until necessary—told the American people, "You never go into battle without every opportunity to prevail, to win, be successful, and to come home safely," his words echoed with credibility and conviction. Powell also knew that in an era of instantaneous news coverage, "You can win the battle or lose the war if you don't handle the story right."

Throughout the '90s, Powell's commanding presence, his pleasant, no-nonsense speaking style, and his unassailable character cut across racial, economic, social, and political lines. His life story—he was raised in the Bronx by Jamaican immigrant parents—illustrated one of America's most deeply held faiths: that hard work, commitment, and perseverance is enough, in the army's words, to "be all that you can be." During his service as the nation's chief military officer, Powell had a 66 percent approval rating, according to a *U.S. News* poll. And when he retired from his 35-year military career in 1993, Powell enjoyed more clout than any other general since Eisenhower.

Following the Gulf War, the media speculated endlessly about the soldier-politician's presidential ambitions, viewing his lauded 1995 memoir, *My American Journey*, as groundwork for a future run. Powell himself, however, remained above the partisan fray, proving reticent about his party affiliation and ambitions throughout the 1992 and 1996 campaigns. Between spending time with his family, delivering speeches, and renovating old Volvos, Powell directed "America's Promise: The Alliance for Youth," an organization encouraging corporate and individual involvement with youth at risk. In Powell's patriotic words, "I have arrived at the point in my life where I am trying to use what I have been given by my nation to help the nation."

A down-to-earth four-star general, Colin Powell (right) helped restore the country's confidence in a military that had gained a reputation for fraud, waste, and failure.

Brand Martha

She was everywhere—on trowels in KMart's gardening department, on recipes for baby food, and on the Internet. Her 27 how-to books on domestic skills sold 9.5 million copies. Her two magazines—*Martha Stewart Living* and *Martha Stewart Weddings*—attracted nearly 10 million readers. Her Web site drew millions of users monthly. At the height of her visibility, Stewart appeared on television 21 times per week.

She had started at age 10 organizing children's parties. She was a model at 13 and did ads during college. In 1967, she became a Wall Street stockbroker who grew orchids in the bathtub and spent weekends restoring a schoolhouse in the Berkshires. In 1972 she quit her job, "deciding that the home [in Westport, Connecticut] was really my place."

From a catering business in the basement of her Connecticut home, the doyenne of domesticity skillfully constructed Martha Stewart Living Omnimedia, a multimedia empire that reached almost every nook and cranny in the culture.

Parodies of her perfectionism abounded. *Is Martha Stuart Living?*, a spoof of her lavishly illustrated magazine, told readers how to whip up a loaf of 90-grain bread and strong-arm the competition at tag sales. A paper-doll book called *Mad About Martha* included accessories to dress Stewart up as Marie Antoinette or as a leather-clad dominatrix. The book parodied the ambitious goals in *Living*'s hallmark monthly calendars with entries such as "Paint Detroit." But Martha Stewart got the last laugh—when the company went public in 1999, Stewart vaulted past Oprah Winfrey to become the nation's wealthiest self-made woman, with an estimated worth of $1.15 billion.

I sacrificed my family, husband. Not my choice. His choice. Now, I'm so happy that it happened. . . . I don't think I would have accomplished what I have if I had stayed married.

When I was a stockbroker, I was outrageous. I wore hot pants. I was one of the few women on Wall Street. . . . I had beautiful long legs.

I don't know why people are so mean about her. Probably because she's so successful.
—Julia Child

Starting from scratch, Martha Stewart (right) whipped up her enormously successful lifestyle business by incorporating television, magazines, books, mailorder, and the Web.

"I find that life is interesting on every level. I read a thing that [wild-man comedian] Sam Kinison said the other day, about how it's tough to live his life so that he has something to talk about. The way I live, it's not a raw life. I have ambitions and disappointments, but I don't want to live a ragged, desperate existence just so I can talk about that. I don't want to necessarily make heavier observations, just better ones. I want to be good."

"I really feel the key to having a successful career in comedy is never taking the bait of stardom per se. If you think you're a star, you're not a comedian anymore, because a comedian is one of us."

"That's my job: to understand what's going on in life, to figure it out. The news, books, magazines and films cover a certain portion of what's going on. But there's a lot of stuff that's not touched on, and that's my job. To tell you the truth, 75 percent of the world is not touched on except by comedians."

"If I wanted to train someone as a comedian, I would make them do lots of proofs. That's what comedy is: a kind of bogus proof. You set up a fallacious premise and then prove it with rigorous logic. It just makes people laugh. You'll find that most of my stuff is based on that system. . . . You must think very rationally on a completely absurd plane."

On the end of Seinfeld, his Emmy-winning TV show: "We've seen a million athletes where you say, 'I wish they didn't do those last two years.' For me, this is all about timing. My life is all about timing. As a comedian, my sense of timing is everything."

"It's a kind of life mission for me. I don't know what the hell I'm trying to accomplish, but I can't stop."

Sein of the Times

One theory of comic inspiration holds that humor is a form of therapy, a safety valve for neurosis. Thus, great comics from Charlie Chaplin and Groucho Marx to Richard Pryor and Roseanne Barr have not so much been making us laugh as keeping themselves from crying or exploding, their jokes the eruptions of a troubled soul.

How, then, to explain the staggering success of Jerry Seinfeld, a man whose only obsession seems to be cereal and whose only deviance is a penchant for neatness? Seinfeld grew up in a happy, middle-class family in Massapequa, Long Island, yet somehow managed to transcend that upbringing. In the comedy-crazed '80s, after waiting tables and peddling light bulbs by phone, the young comedian—along with Jay Leno, Garry Shandling, and Steven Wright—broke through the ranks. So by the time the '90s arrived, Seinfeld was a successful club comedian—working 300 nights per year—and ended the decade with the kind of fame and fortune usually reserved for the biggest rock and movie stars.

There was nothing earthshaking about his material. It was always clean and always rooted in everyday experience. ("What's the point of helmets in skydiving?" or "They say Tide cleans bloodstains. I say if you've got a T-shirt with bloodstains, then maybe laundry isn't your biggest problem.") Seinfeld was "Mr. Generic," in the words of one critic, and while that broadened his fan base, it also opened him up to occasional criticism.

Seinfeld found his edge and honed it by teaming with fellow stand-up Larry David. The pair came up with the idea that became *Seinfeld*, the most successful TV sitcom of the '90s, while hanging out in a New York deli late one night after performing. The more cerebral and neurotic David provided the show with dark comic undertones. Like Seinfeld's club routines, though, *Seinfeld*, with its star surrounded by a colorful TV cast of dysfunctional characters, was essentially "about nothing."

In 1998, the year *Seinfeld* went into syndication, the comedian earned $225 million, making him that year's top breadwinner in all of show business. He still insisted, though, that the biggest day of his life was the day he could finally say, "I'm a comedian. That's all I do."

Jerry Seinfeld (right) evokes his incessant paranoia. His observational humor made the unbelievable believable.

A Man with a Plan

Newt Gingrich shot like a rogue meteor from being a Georgia college history professor to being Speaker of the House in the U.S. Congress. When cable network C-SPAN installed cameras in the House chamber, Congressman Gingrich quickly turned the medium to his advantage. After other representatives had gone home for the day, he took the podium to pitch his ideas for a Republican revolution. Until Democratic Speaker of the House Tip O'Neill ordered the cameras to pan the hall, it had not occurred to the public that Newt was railing against Democratic domination of Congress to an empty chamber.

Although Gingrich became "the most disliked member of Congress," he almost single-handedly galvanized a divisive Republican Party behind a single GOP platform. His so-called Contract with America—with reforms ranging from a balanced budget to term limits for elected officials—seized on the public's dissatisfaction with Bill Clinton and ushered a record number of freshmen into the House. For the first time in 40 years, Republicans controlled Congress. For this astonishing feat, *Time* magazine named Newt Gingrich "Man of the Year" in 1995.

But as some fellow Republicans soon realized, Gingrich preferred grand concepts and visionary ideas to daily politics. He spent four years as the Speaker of the House before abruptly resigning after the 1998 mid-term election. The same qualities that led to his rapid ascent as the leader of the "Republican Reformation"—arrogance, militance, and nerve—eroded his support and sowed rancor in Republican ranks. Democrats gleefully came to view him as the perfect adversary and his own worst enemy, prone to pettiness and vain gaffes.

"My strength and my weakness is that I see normally impersonal events vividly and personally."

"I am too intense, and ironically, I am too unsteady. You know I take risks, and I say things that probably a more studied, careful, planned approach would avoid."

"When you are a backbencher, you use very strong language—and this is still a weakness of my current style. If you are in everybody's living room virtually every night having a conversation, that intensity of language is counterproductive."

"There is a part of me that passionately wants to be a teacher, and I am not in a teaching job. And so I have consistently, all year, said things that make no sense for the Speaker of the House. They would be terrific comments from an analyst or a political-science teacher, but they just did not make any sense. I am trying to think through how to remain a teacher without being self-destructive."

Speaker of the House Newt Gingrich appears at a gathering of the Christian Coalition, August 14, 1996.

"The success you achieve on a professional level can have nothing and everything to do with your personal life."

"I don't walk around thinking, I light up the screen, OOH! You still wake up in the morning and say, 'What am I supposed to do in this scene?'"

"My life is really lovely, and it is a culmination of all of my choices. So I'm really proud of it. I feel like I made very good choices."

"It's bizarre to deal with reports in the press about my romantic life. . . . I've read flat-out lies so hideous they made me cry."

"An actor friend once told me, 'I'd hate to be you.' And I said, 'It's actually kinda great being me. I have a remarkable, spectacular, amazing life for which I am so grateful. It's the best-kept secret in town.'"

"Julia's still vulnerable . . . she's a sensitive girl. But I think she's learned a lot about handling the life of a star."
—Garry Marshall, director

"Julia is touched by something, a zest and life force you just want to be around. She became a huge star early, which a lot of people don't survive. She's managed to get through it with her soul intact."
—Steven Soderbergh, director

"Julia's very beautiful, she's very bright, she's very everything."
—Eric Roberts, actor, brother

"Despite all the complexity and chaos that appear to exist in her life, she's also a very simple person. Simple in the most beautiful ways: generous, soulful, giving, humorous, loving—all those things that are important to me."
—Benjamin Bratt, boyfriend, actor

"She's got the je ne sais quoi."
—Jeffrey Katzenberg, Dreamworks executive

Pretty Woman

The buzz surrounding Julia Roberts heightened to a roar with the 1990 release of *Pretty Woman*, the boy-meets-call-girl-with-heart-of-gold romantic comedy that garnered more than $460 million worldwide and a Best Actress Oscar nomination for Roberts. A virtual unknown just two years before, Roberts had captured the public's heart in 1989 with her stirring performance (officially acknowledged with a Best Supporting Actress nomination) in the tearjerker *Steel Magnolias*. She was just 22 at the time.

By turns elegant starlet and shy girl from Smyrna, Georgia, Roberts appealed to a wide range of audiences. Her endearing underdog quality, ever-twinkling eyes, and quick, broad smile made her appear more accessible than most Hollywood stars. She had the innocent charm of Audrey Hepburn, the tentative feminist impulses of Diane Keaton, and the bankability, if not depth, of Meryl Streep. As one reviewer described her, Roberts was someone "women liked and wanted to be, and men liked and wanted to have."

Inundated with scripts and media attention following *Pretty Woman*, Roberts made four films in one year and catapulted herself into the status of Hollywood's highest-paid actress, commanding $7 million per film. Such quick fame at such a young age comes with a price, though. What intrigued the public even more than Roberts's onscreen roles was her turbulent private life. She called off her wedding to actor Kiefer Sutherland days before their scheduled 1991 nuptials and dated a number of actors before marrying singer-songwriter Lyle Lovett in 1993 after a three-week courtship. (The couple would divorce 21 months later.)

During this time, endlessly probing media and insatiable fans drove Roberts into a Garbo-like seclusion for nearly two years, until the '93 release of *The Pelican Brief*. The film earned $100 million domestically, but Roberts would not reach those box-office heights again until the '97 hit *My Best Friend's Wedding*. The public quickly forgave Roberts her string of mediocre films in the mid-'90s (as well as her retreat) and welcomed her back into superstardom. Roberts closed the decade with a trio of blockbusters: *Stepmom*, *Notting Hill*, and *Runaway Bride*.

Off-camera, Julia Roberts (right) took her dazzling smile abroad to places like Haiti and India as a representative for UNICEF and other charitable organizations.

"Night after night, year after year, he just carries this team. He never avoids it, never shirks it."
—John Paxson, teammate

"You don't know what he's going to do. He goes right, left, over you, around and under you. He twists, he turns. And you know he's going to get that shot off. You just don't know when and how."
—Michael Cooper of the Los Angeles Lakers

"He is the most awesome player in the NBA. . . . I couldn't believe someone could do that against the Boston Celtics."
—Larry Bird, after Jordan scored 63 points

"I cannot imagine anyone playing any better."
—Bill Russell

"As a golfer, you're used to seeing celebrities on the golf course, but Michael is at a whole different level. This is great. Just watching people react to him is incredible."
—David Duval, professional golfer

"At first, Michael and I took a wait-and-see attitude toward each other. I didn't want to become too familiar with him, as some of my predecessors had been, because I knew I had to win his respect. It wasn't until we won our first championship—and he could see that the changes I had implemented actually worked—that our relationship opened up and we developed a strong partnership."
—Phil Jackson, coach

"He said he never was so tired in his life. He said it was his hardest year and he felt he had to carry the team in the Finals more than he'd ever had. He was totally exhausted, mentally and physically."
—Jerry Reinsdorf, Bulls owner, in 1999

"This time, I know from a career standpoint I've accomplished everything I could. I don't have the challenges I've had in the past to proceed. This is a perfect time for me to walk away from the game. I'm at peace with that."
—Michael Jordan on his 1999 retirement

His Airness

As high as he soared, as unerringly as he launched his jumper, Michael Jordan's greatest gift, the one thing that separated him from that army of breathtaking athletes known as the NBA, was his will to win. On the golf course, at the gaming tables, and even at Bulls' practices, where Jordan's taunts are supposed to have broken the spirit of at least one teammate, Jordan simply had to win.

And so he did—again, and again, and again. In the course of his 13-season career Jordan won 10 scoring titles and averaged 31.5 points per game, the highest in league history. Five times he was voted Most Valuable Player. Most important of all, Jordan led his Chicago Bulls to six championships in eight years. After watching Jordan score a play-off record 63 points against the Boston Celtics in 1986, Hall of Famer Larry Bird said simply, "I think he's God disguised as Michael Jordan."

He was handsome, charismatic, and dignified, but Jordan was not perfect. There were revelations of gambling and of huge debts run up in the company of questionable men. Even more troubling to some, he remained as fiercely apolitical as Muhammad Ali had been revolutionary. When Jordan was asked to campaign for Harvey Gantt, an African American running for the U.S. Senate against ultraconservative Jesse Helms in Jordan's home state of North Carolina, he refused, pointing out that "Republicans buy sneakers too."

When Jordan retired on January 13, 1999, he was praised almost everywhere as the greatest basketball player in history. But like Babe Ruth and Muhammad Ali before him, Jordan transcended sport and became something of a myth. He single-handedly lifted the NBA to a level of popularity it is only now, with no Air apparent, beginning fully to appreciate.

With endorsement contracts with Nike—which netted him $6 million in 1990 for his fabulously popular $125 a pair Air Jordan sneakers—Gatorade, McDonald's, and Wheaties, Jordan was welcomed into American homes. "Be like Mike," urged one ad campaign. But anyone who has watched a reel of Jordan highlights knows that no one could ever seriously expect to do that.

The uncontested master of the hardwood, Michael Jordan (right) also set style trends: When he ordered his uniform shorts to be cut long and baggy, the entire league converted; when he shaved his head, bald suddenly became beautiful.

Talk Radio's
Enfant Terrible

By the time Howard Stern's oddly endearing feature film, *Private Parts*, hit theaters in 1997, talk radio's controversial, potty-mouthed "shock jock" had already grown on millions of daily listeners, "like a fungus," as he himself put it. What struck some New York radio audiences as an embarassingly myopic sideshow of bigotry, racism, sexually charged jokes, and gutter-quality humor had become a national mainstream phenomenon.

Indeed, it was hard to determine whether Stern was a portent of cultural doom or simply an envelope-pushing comedian. In any case, Stern, who alternated between being disarmingly self-effacing and mercilessly degrading of others, attracted an audience so large he changed the course of radio history.

His popularity helped ignite the explosive growth of talk radio, a medium that spawned the archconservative political gabber Rush Limbaugh and the hardball dispenser of advice Dr. Laura (Schlessinger). In the arena of tasteless entertainment, though, Stern had no peer. He regaled fans with regular features such as Fartman, Butt Bongo, and Dial-a-Date. When he crossed over into late-night TV, on CBS, the self-proclaimed "King of all Media" brought his radio show and its motley guests—including Ku Klux Klan members, strippers, and Hank the Angry Drunken Dwarf, among others—intact to the visual medium. The result made *Saturday Night Live* look like a church social.

"John McCain wouldn't be a candidate if he had just been a better pilot."

"The only bad thing about the Rodney King incident is that Clarence Thomas wasn't in the back seat."

"What I try to do with humor is show the absurdities of the differences between people."

"It's true, as in the movie, that my father yelled at me all the time—and called me 'MORON' and 'STUPID.' Making this movie . . . is my way of proving to my father that I'm finally OK."

"Howard was a very sensitive child." —Ray Stern, Howard's mother

---

Howard Stern (center) strikes a typically egomaniacal pose among his favorite admirers, sparsely-clad women. One critic called Stern's popularity part of the "dumbing down of America."

A Line
in the Sand

★

AMERICA, IRAQ, AND THE NEW WORLD ORDER

The end of the Cold War prompted President George Bush to speak optimistically of a New World Order in which the superpowers would shift their focus to greater humanitarian concerns. But when Saddam Hussein's Iraqi army invaded the small, oil-rich nation of Kuwait on August 2, 1990, President Bush marshaled a global alliance of a very different sort to protect the world's vital oil reserves. The president's catch phrase had taken on a decidedly strident tone.

Bush's first action, taken six days after the Iraqi invasion, was to send American troops to the border between Kuwait and Saudi Arabia. Declaring that "a line has been drawn in the sand," Bush made it clear he would tolerate no threat to America's interests in Saudi Arabia. Then began the hard work of forming the multinational coalition the president would need to facilitate—and legitimize—the ouster of the Iraqis from Kuwaiti soil.

OPERATION
DESERT STORM

By October 25, 300,000 Allied troops from 19 nations were stationed in Saudi Arabia under the command of U.S. general H. Norman Schwarzkopf. Their service was not easy: Constant water was needed to combat the heat and much of their training focused on the horrifying possibility of chemical and biological warfare. For many there was an even greater hardship: the need to sit and wait, anxious and uncertain about what lay ahead. Operation Desert Storm, a name popularized by buttons *(inset)* worn by supporters at home, was still months away.

One casualty of the Gulf War was the environment, as hundreds of burning Kuwaiti oil wells—some bombed, some set on fire by retreating Iraqi soldiers—darken the skies (left).

The Butcher of Baghdad

While Saddam Hussein always resented the West's meddling in the Middle East, he was not above using American interests to enhance his position. During the '80s, as Americans quaked in terror over the possibility of the fundamentalist revolution in Iran spreading throughout the region, he was able to get significant backing from the United States in his war against the Ayatollah. But when he invaded Kuwait and threatened America's vital interests, Hussein presumed too much.

The stakes were high indeed: A victory in Kuwait and Saudi Arabia would have made Hussein the preeminent nationalist of the Arab world and put 45 percent of the world's oil reserves in Iraqi hands. Little wonder that the West was concerned. Faced with a January 15, 1991, deadline to pull out of Kuwait, Hussein responded with characteristic bluster, demonizing Bush and the United States and promising the "mother of all battles." He would soon learn that the Allies were not bluffing.

During the Gulf War, politicians cast Hussein as an evil madman. Some of this was predictable wartime propaganda, the sort of rhetoric that has always been applied to America's enemies. But in the case of Hussein, there was much to support the aspersions. When he was 21, Hussein reportedly murdered his brother-in-law, who had been a political opponent. In the summer of 1979, the same year he became the Iraqi president, Hussein executed approximately 500 top Baathists—members of his own party—to consolidate his power. And in 1988 he used chemical weapons to crush a rebellion in the Kurdish town of Halabja. Clearly, the facts supported the impression of Hussein as one who appreciated the use of brute force. Such ruthlessness, combined with a reputation for paranoia and unpredictability, made him a man to watch closely in the Middle East.

> "He is neither a strategist . . . nor is he a tactician, nor is he a general, nor is he a soldier. Other than that, he's a great military man."

General H. Norman Schwarzkopf, when asked his impressions of Saddam Hussein's military strategy

A commanding portrait of Saddam Hussein covers a wall in Baghdad (above) one year after the invasion. Hussein (opposite) rallies 10,000 students two months after Iraq's retreat from Kuwait.

Equipped with infrared radar, the U.S. Air Force's F-15 Eagle fighter (above) could produce a map of its target on a cockpit display before reaching the area. Iraqi air defense responds to Allied bombing (right).

Video Game Warfare

I t's like a Nintendo game," said CNN's Bernard Shaw, as he watched a videotape of a laser-guided "smart" bomb zeroing in on and hitting its target in Baghdad. Viewers at home marveled too, as images released by the military showed missiles making sharp turns or zipping down chimneys to reach their targets.

Thus was the American public introduced to a shocking and destructive type of blitzkrieg warfare that featured a new generation of hi-tech weaponry. Bombs could adjust their courses allegedly to hit within three feet of their targets. Stealth bombers and fighter planes operated virtually undetected over the skies of Iraq. Night-vision equipment provided accuracy around the clock. And the Patriot antimissile system intercepted the vast majority of enemy missiles before impact.

The result of all this wizardry was stunning: After eight years of desert war experience with Iran and boasting the world's fourth largest army, Iraq was nevertheless brought to its knees by the Allies' rain of terror. During the opening 38-day air assault known as Operation Desert Storm, the Allies eliminated the eyes and ears of the Iraqi war machine by targeting strategic communications and radar systems. By the time the ground assault

During the first 24 hours of bombing, 30 computer-designed F-117A stealth fighters (top) allegedly hit 37 "high-value targets," collapsing Baghdad's sophisticated air defense system and virtually destroying Iraq's ability to coordinate its firepower; carefully orchestrated video clips of targets and bombing (above) demonstrated the precision of Allied attacks to television viewers around the world.

got under way, the Iraqis were powerless to resist. While the Allied leadership was receiving information directly from the battlefield via satellite communications and making instantaneous adjustments, the Iraqis were largely cut off from one another and immobilized. After only 100 hours of ground combat, the war was over.

When the fighting stopped, only 148 American soldiers had lost their lives, as compared to vague estimates ranging from 8,000 to 100,000 Iraqis. Another 15,000

Americans reported suffering from Gulf War Syndrome, a baffling combination of symptoms that included fatigue, muscle and joint pains, headaches, memory loss, skin rash, diarrhea, and sleep disturbances.

Chastened but not removed from power, Hussein continued to haunt the region at decade's end, functioning as the x factor in Middle East politics, an unpredictable despot whose actions frequently bordered on the irrational. No amount of technological expertise could change that.

General H. Norman Schwarzkopf briefs the press; his straightforward, no-nonsense style earned him the respect of journalists as well as the American people.

"An American citizen is entitled to ask, 'What are they trying to hide?' "

Former CBS anchorman Walter Cronkite, on the unprecedented press restrictions during the Gulf War

A Blinkered Press

In the early hours of January 17, 1991, three Cable News Network journalists crawled around their Baghdad hotel room on their hands and knees as bombs exploded in the city around them. For 16 straight hours, they described the sights and sounds of war live via satellite to a captivated worldwide audience. CNN's prime-time viewership exploded that night from 560,000 to 11.4 million and helped establish it as *the* Gulf War source. CNN's coverage and in-depth reporting by the other networks introduced the names and faces of the conflict to the entire world. Reporters such as NBC's Arthur Kent and CNN's Peter Arnett *(inset)* became household names. The handsome Kent, nicknamed the "Scud Stud," even inspired legions of female admirers to create fan clubs.

Although CNN and other news organizations sometimes made conducting the war more difficult for both sides, wall-to-wall news proved to be the greatest weapon yet in the battle for public opinion. Nobody understood the media's impact better than American decision makers, many of whom had watched in horror as hard-nosed, often grisly coverage of Vietnam

had turned the nation against the war. Determined to avoid a similar disaster in the Gulf, military leaders heavily restricted press access to the conflict, forcing the vast majority of journalists to rely on the military's highly partisan briefings for information about the course of the war. Only well after the fact, when the conflict had long departed America's front pages, did the nation learn the truth: The F-117's reported 37 strikes turned out to be only 21 actual hits, low-cost A-10s performed as well as high-cost F-117s at night, and many of the so-called smart bombs proved dumb, missing their targets and killing as many as 2,300 Iraqi civilians.

As Richard Haass, a Middle East expert on the National Security Council, said, "It [television] really became at times our chief tool—and I don't mean this in a cynical way—for selling policy."

Reporters scramble to take advantage of
one of the military's prearranged
"pools"—groups of journalists allowed
controlled access to the war—which for
most of the press corps represented their
only chance to witness real soldiers in
action in the field.

The Soviet Collapse

★

THE SECOND RUSSIAN REVOLUTION

The world looked on in amazement as strong symbols of the Soviet Union came crashing down. The December 9, 1991, headline of the *New York Times* noted one of the key political moments of the day before. The formerly secretive and closed Soviet society was undergoing dramatic changes.

Mikhail Gorbachev, who had taken power in 1985, had introduced his revolutionary programs of political, economic, and social liberalization. But his initiatives set off unintended consequences: civil war erupting between Armenians and Azerbaijanis, Lithuanians declaring independence, and even Russia moving toward autonomy. Fearing the Soviet Union's breakup and the reaction from military hard-liners, he ordered troops to the Baltics, authorized patrols to maintain order, and replaced his original team of reformers with hacks from the Party's Central Committee.

Despite charges from some that Gorbachev was changing too much too fast, others, including the fiery Russian president Boris Yeltsin, complained the reforms weren't going far enough. The stage was set for the Soviet Union's next major drama.

On August 24, 1991, Latvians gather around a recently dismantled statue of Lenin (left), which once stood in the center of the Latvian capital of Riga. An onlooker holds the national flag of the new Russian Federation.

Lithuanians defiantly wave their beloved national flag during a 1990 demonstration for independence from the Soviet Union.

United States president George Bush and Soviet leader Mikhail Gorbachev greet each other at the 1991 Moscow Summit.

"How it will end we do not know, but there is no turning back now."

Sergei Zalygin, editor of the crusading literary monthly *Novy Mir*

The Coup That Shook the World

In July 1991, hard-liners requested support of dramatic action to end the disorder caused by Gorbachev's reform attempts. Western observers rightly began to anticipate a coup, which came on Monday, August 19, 1991, one day before Gorbachev's scheduled signing of a new union treaty that would limit the Kremlin's control.

A group went to Gorbachev's vacation house in the Crimea and placed him under house arrest as a committee of eight seized power. But the coup would prove to be inept and curiously half-hearted. The conspirators failed to shut down the country's communications and press, they neglected to arrest popular potential enemies of the coup, and they even said complimentary things about Gorbachev and held out the possibility of working with him again. Further, they overlooked strategic troop placement and gave orders to avoid confrontation.

The plotters thought that they could easily win over the people, given the economic collapse that had made Gorbachev unpopular and the long tradition of Russian submissiveness to authority. But under Gorbachev the people had grown in their newfound freedom, and the coup became an old-style attempt in a new-style society. In the new social and political atmosphere, President Boris Yeltsin of Russia and presidents of other Soviet republics declared the coup unconstitutional. At 12:30 p.m. on Monday, before the coup could even get fully under way, Yeltsin climbed atop an armored truck outside Russia's parliament building to assume command and to call for a general strike to thwart the coup. His appearance inspired public demonstrations throughout the country—even military leaders defected.

By Wednesday, with only three casualties, the mismanaged coup fell apart, having instead intensified the move toward democracy and decentralization. The coup had become, as some called it, surreal.

Jubilant protesters climb aboard tanks to celebrate their victory as the tide turns against the plotters of the 1991 coup to remove Gorbachev.

United States president Bill Clinton and Russian president Boris Yeltsin share a toast (above) during a dinner at the Russian embassy in Washington, D.C., on September 28, 1994.

"Yeltsin is at his best not when he's governing, but when he's at the head of an angry crowd."

Analyst Dimitri Simes

A Pizza Hut sign (above) in Moscow in January 1992 signals the dramatic changes in Russia and its economy.

Bumpy Road to Freedom

B oris Yeltsin was elected Russian president on June 12, 1991, in the country's first democratic presidential elections (after Russia adopted the Declaration of Sovereignty on June 12, 1990—its Independence Day). During the August 1991 coup attempt, Yeltsin acted decisively and emerged as the country's leading political figure.

In the coup's aftermath, Yeltsin banned the Communist Party. Gorbachev resigned as head the party on August 24, 1991, one day after the coup failed. On December 8, 1991, in Minsk, Yeltsin and the presidents of Belarus and Ukraine signed a treaty that replaced the central government of the old Soviet Union with a decentralized community of independent nations. And finally, on December 24, 1991, Russia took over the USSR's seat in the U.N.—the next day Gorbachev resigned as Soviet president and the USSR formally ceased to exist.

Yeltsin boldly led the former Soviet Union down the path that Gorbachev had feared to walk. Immediately, he recognized Estonia, Latvia, and Lithuania's right to go their own way. He permitted the residents of Leningrad to resume calling their city St. Petersburg, a name that had been forbidden since the era of Soviet strongman Joseph Stalin.

Some Western and Russian leaders dismissed the hard-drinking

Russian president Boris Yeltsin raises his arm in triumph, having rallied the resistance that helped prevent the Communists from ousting Gorbachev in the 1991 coup d'état.

While record numbers in their country suffer poverty-stricken conditions, affluent members of the younger generation dance the night away at a club in the new Russia.

The Russian Lottery premieres on October 21, 1992, as Western cultural influence continues to grow.

Yeltsin as a buffoon and an opportunist. But Yeltsin enjoyed a solid relationship with the Russian populace, who saw him as one of them, a man who frequently rode subways and commuter buses.

Yeltsin continued to push for a new, democratic constitution and for economic reforms intended to transform the sluggish Soviet system into a free market economy. Describing his approach as "shock therapy," Yeltsin urged his nation toward increased privatization. The result was skyrocketing inflation that depleted savings and devalued salaries. Prices for consumer goods rose dramatically. Per capita income decreased from 43 percent that of the United States in 1989 to 10 percent in 1995. The birth rate declined, life expectancy fell—even per capita caloric intake dropped.

During Russia's first five years of independence, industrial and agricultural output fell by more than 40 percent, a more precipitous drop than America experienced during the Great Depression in the 1930s. Unemployment ran between 13 and 15 percent, and the gap between the richest and poorest widened significantly. Far from encouraging a new middle class, such economic stratification blocked social progress, as most of the new elite had held political or economic status in the old order. Further, political instability and corrupt banking discouraged foreign investment. Widespread organized crime produced a surge in contract killings and a sharp increase in the homicide rate.

Meanwhile, the republic of Chechnya, which had always sought independence and which leaders from the czars and Stalin through Yeltsin had found difficult to manage, again attempted to break away. Yeltsin decided to assert control over Chechnya, and Russia invaded on December 11, 1994. Initial Russian air strikes only served to strengthen Chechen resistance, and the once mighty Russian army proved incompetent. The Chechens, on the other hand, many of whom were veterans of the Soviet army, worked effectively in small, mobile groups. By the end of the bloody, largely inconclusive separatist war, some 100,000 lives had been lost.

Russian military vehicles head to positions north of the Chechen capital of Grozny.

Despite the fiasco in Chechnya and the failure of his reform program, Yeltsin was reelected in 1996. But his waning health was becoming an issue. Yeltsin had suffered a heart attack prior to the elections. According to insiders, he had also become subject to depression and despair and was easily manipulated by those around him. As his health deteriorated, he became increasingly withdrawn.

On December 31, 1999, with Russian troops again moving on the Chechen capital of Grozny, Boris Yeltsin announced, "Today, on the last day of the outgoing century, I am resigning." Before handing leadership over to 47-year-old Prime Minister Vladimir Putin, he apologized for his failures and concluded, "Be happy. You deserve happiness."

A sign of Russia's economic crisis, a young girl (right) begs on a Moscow street in 1994.

A Baby Boomer at the Helm

★

THE CLINTON PRESIDENCY

E ven as a young child, he had an enthusiasm for people and wanted to help them fulfill their dreams. But when William Jefferson Clinton shook hands with President
John F. Kennedy in the Rose Garden at age 16 *(inset)*, his life changed and the presidency
became his burning desire.

Toward that end, he assiduously developed credentials. A
Rhodes scholar, he worked to impress listeners with his grasp
of arcane economic detail and intricate governmental issues.
He burnished his image further by stressing his classically
humble beginnings—a father dead before his birth, an alco-
holic stepfather, and a hometown called Hope. Good looking,
empathetic, and startlingly bright, he was charisma incarnate.
Arkansas attorney general at 30 and governor at 32, Clinton
was only 46 when he became the nation's 42nd chief executive. He presided over unprecedented peacetime prosperity,
but his two-term tenure was marred by scandal. As Republi-
can nemesis Newt Gingrich once remarked, "Bill Clinton has all of FDR's skills—but none
of the iron." Only history can decide the fairness of that description.

*The newly elected president and first lady celebrate at an election night rally in Little Rock (left). The
campaign used Fleetwood Mac's 1977 hit "Don't Stop (Thinking About Tomorrow)" as a theme song.*

Born to Campaign

Getting to the White House demanded all of Bill Clinton's youthful vigor, persistence, and political savvy. During the primaries he had to dodge accusations aimed at his character: He had evaded the Vietnam draft, and he had tried marijuana, though he insisted he hadn't inhaled. He even went on TV with his wife, Hillary, to counter allegations of a 12-year extramarital affair with former nightclub singer Gennifer Flowers.

Clinton then faced a Republican incumbent considered unbeatable. Basking in the glow of the Gulf War vic-

> **"The foremost thing about this man is that he loves people . . . and he wants that love back."**
>
> Betsey Wright, Bill Clinton's former chief of staff in Arkansas, during the '92 campaign

tory, President George Bush enjoyed the highest approval ratings ever recorded. When computer entrepreneur Ross Perot—like Bush, a distinguished veteran of the navy— jumped in as a third-party candidate, Clinton plummeted to third in the polls. But Bush, already saddled with his broken pledge "Read my lips: no new taxes," soon lost focus, allowing right-wing extremists to dominate the GOP convention. Perot, concerned about his own and his family's privacy, dropped out of the race.

Clinton, the consummate campaigner, hugged everyone in sight, played the saxophone on late-night TV, and

CLINTON
A CURE FOR THE BLUES

plied the heartland on a bus with his V.P. nominee, Al Gore. Sticking to the theme posted on the wall of his Little Rock war room—"The economy, stupid"—he proffered solutions to end the recession and the crippling 7.5 percent rate of unemployment. The result was close but Clinton squeaked by with 43 percent of the popular vote.

Bill Clinton addresses supporters in St. Louis (left) on July 22, 1992, the last day of a six-day, eight-state cross-country bus tour. Clinton listens to voters (above) in a doughnut shop in Hampton, New Hampshire, during the 1992 Democratic primary race, the very embodiment of one of his famous slogans, "I feel your pain."

The Clintons and Gores relax inside their cross-country campaign bus in October 1992 (below). A campaign button (opposite) shows the sax-playing Clinton.

Grand Visions and Indecision

Clinton and attorney general designee Zoë Baird confer at a news conference. Baird would be forced to withdraw in the so-called Nannygate scandal.

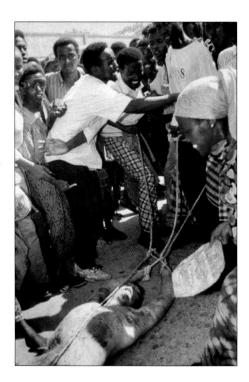

The abuse of a dead U.S. military airman in Mogadishu, Somalia, presents a grisly image that upset Americans back home. He was one of five Americans killed on the first day of the UN assault.

Sure-footed as a campaigner, Clinton stumbled in his early days as president. His first missteps stemmed from his stated desire to have a cabinet so diverse that it "looked like America." He was determined to appoint the nation's first female attorney general, but he was forced to drop his first two nominees because of questions raised about their nannies: One had hired illegal immigrants, and the other had failed to pay her employee's social security taxes. Clinton's attempt to fulfill a campaign promise to lift the ban on homosexuals in military ended in the "Don't Ask, Don't Tell" compromise that satisfied neither the commanders of the military branches nor the gay community.

"The will to please is so prevalent that it is interfering with his effectiveness."

Unnamed White House adviser on Clinton's management style

His clumsiness extended to foreign policy as well, even though, ironically, Clinton's undergraduate major at Georgetown University had been international relations. In Somalia, a humanitarian effort launched in the last days of the Bush Administration turned sour. Despite Clinton's best efforts to deal with a situation he had inherited, 30 American servicemen died. Television images of a fallen GI being dragged through the streets brought home the perils of even the best-intentioned foreign intervention. Chastened, Clinton refused to intervene in Rwanda, despite widespread genocide there that resulted in at least one million deaths.

Clinton was tripped up most conspicuously by healthcare reform. More than 30 million Americans lacked medical insurance in the early '90s. To those hard workers who had fallen through the healthcare cracks, candidate Clinton had promised expanded coverage. In fact, affordable healthcare for every man, woman, and child was the linchpin of his broad platform for change.

But critics accused him of nepotism when he named Hillary to lead the

First Lady Hillary Clinton addresses a health-care reform rally (top); a clock behind her demonstrates one person losing healthcare every 1.17 seconds.

drive to reform the nation's health insurance industry. Intellect and drive aside, she was neither an elected official nor an appointee subject to Senate approval. The first lady's planning process quickly drew criticism for being secretive; the plan itself was so complex, once it emerged, that few could understand it. The insurance industry mounted such an effective lobbying campaign—including shrewd TV commercials featuring the fictional couple "Harry and Louise" discussing, in oversimplified terms, the alleged pitfalls of the proposed program—that Congress did not even have to go through the motions of voting the reform package down. It died on its own.

By the end of Clinton's first year in office, many Americans were wondering, along with *Time (inset),* just how ineffective and unpopular this president could become.

A Conservative Revolution, Almost

C linton's early missteps helped set the stage for the ascent of Newt Gingrich, the Republican leader in the House of Representatives. His conservative revolution would produce a showdown with the president and a shutdown of the government but would ultimately disintegrate as America returned to its usual moderate roots.

A political bomb thrower but also a gifted strategist, Gingrich crafted a manifesto for his party's candidates in the 1994 Congressional elections. His 10-point "Contract with America" called for tax cuts, term limits for elected officials, and a constitutional

House Republican freshmen walk to a December 21, 1995, news conference at the Capitol Christmas tree; they called on the president to accept their balanced budget proposal in observance of the holidays.

CLOSED Due to President's Refusal to Sign Interior Bill.

Bob Livingston, Republican representative from Louisiana, carries a sign outside the National Gallery. Many people were unable to attend special art exhibits and visit national parks.

At a January 1995 Capitol Hill press conference (above), Newt Gingrich holds up a copy of his "Contract with America."

amendment requiring a balanced budget. The contract's conservative vision energized Republican candidates all across the nation.

Not a single Republican incumbent lost, and the GOP took control of the Senate, the House (for the first time in 40 years), and the majority of statehouses. Suddenly Newt Gingrich, onetime political outsider, was the Speaker of the House.

Gingrich and his colleagues quickly set out to shrink the government and enact their Contract into law. But they overestimated the conservatism of the electorate, and by threatening Medicare, student loans, and other programs dear to the middle class, they unwittingly played into the hands of Clinton, who was able to portray himself as the stalwart defender of common decency against the wild-eyed excesses of the radical Republicans in Congress. In an impasse over the budget in August 1995, "nonessential" federal workers were furloughed for nearly a month and a host of federal facilities were shut down. Gingrich, caught in the public backlash, later confessed that he and his fellow firebrands had underestimated the president's political resilience. Clinton had done it again.

Presidency in Motion

Despite the severe Democratic setback in the 1994 midterm elections, Clinton spearheaded an impressive array of successful policies and legislative initiatives. He made good on his vow to diversify the government by appointing more women and minorities than any of his predecessors. He won a ban on assault weapons and pushed through the Brady Bill, which called for background checks and waiting periods for handgun sales. He committed federal dollars for 100,000 more policemen and an equal number of additional schoolteachers. He increased the earned income tax credit for the working poor, expanded Head Start, and inaugurated AmeriCorps *(inset),* a domestic version of the Peace Corps. Internationally, he promoted economic globalization with measures such as the North American Free Trade Agreement (NAFTA), he worked to forge peace in the Middle East, Northern Ireland, and Bosnia, and he helped block Serbian aggression in Kosovo.

Ironically, two of the most important landmarks of the Clinton era derived from the Republican agenda. Radical changes in the federal welfare system imposed time limits and work requirements on mothers, ending what Clinton called "welfare as we know it." Balanced budget agreements with Congress led to two straight years of surplus and the first reduction of the national debt in nearly three decades. Clinton's accommodation on both issues stemmed from a strategy in which he sought to position himself in the political center. Under his stewardship, unemployment plunged to 4.3 percent, the lowest level in 29 years, and the economy experienced the longest period of expansion in the nation's history. His missteps now forgotten, the American people came to see their president as a man who got things done.

Clinton reads a book of nursery rhymes to elementary schoolchildren (above). His many efforts to assist children included the creation of a $24 billion Children's Health Insurance Program to provide medical coverage for up to five million children and a tax of $500 per child for 27 million lower-income families.

President Bill Clinton signs the Brady Bill in a November 1993 White House ceremony. Seated at President Clinton's right is James Brady, the presidential press secretary who was shot and disabled in a 1981 assassination attempt on Ronald Reagan. Standing (left to right) are Vice President Al Gore, Attorney General Janet Reno, and Brady's wife, Sarah.

Yitzhak Rabin and Yassir Arafat shake hands at the White House on September 13, 1993, after signing the peace accord between Israel and the Palestine Liberation Organization.

Lewinsky arrives for a second day of grand jury testimony in August 1998. In what she considered a sign of support, Clinton wore to the hearing one of the ties Lewinsky had given him.

Surviving Scandals from Day One

President Clinton's embrace of Monica Lewinsky (left) at a celebration with White House staff after his reelection became the scandal's most enduring image.

C linton's record of accomplishments, especially his economic success, led to his decisive 1996 reelection over former Republican Senate majority leader and World War II veteran Bob Dole. But criticisms and allegations of impropriety continued over matters ranging from the trivial, such as his firing of seven White House travel office employees, to the mysterious, as in the shocking suicide of his deputy counsel and boyhood friend, Vincent Foster. But no scandal threatened to undo both the president's record and his reputation more than his sexual relationship with Monica Lewinsky, a 22-year-old White House intern when the relationship began in November 1995.

After Lewinsky's internship ended in April 1996 she became employed at the Pentagon, where she innocently, but fatefully, confided details of Oval Office trysts to her new Pentagon colleague, Linda Tripp. Tripp, by no means a Clinton supporter, had secretly recorded 20 hours of Lewinsky's late-night telephone confessions. Armed with her tapes, Tripp offered them as ammunition to the lawyers for Paula Jones, a former Arkansas state employee who was suing the president for sexual harassment, charging that he had asked for oral sex in a Little Rock hotel room in 1991 and then failed to promote her after she declined.

Meanwhile, an old real estate venture known as Whitewater continued to hound the president. Back in the 1980s Bill and Hillary Clinton had entered a partnership with friends and political supporters James and Susan McDougal to develop homesites on a 230-acre tract along Arkansas's White River. The enterprise had failed, as did a savings and loan run by James McDougal, eventually costing taxpayers $47 million to bail out. Lingering questions about the Clintons' involvement led to the appointment of an independent counsel with broad powers to investigate this and other possibly related improprieties. Whitewater, it turned out, was just a tributary, albeit a major one, to Clinton's river of scandals.

In late 1998 the issues of womanizing and Whitewater converged as the evasive president was pitted against the relentless independent counsel Kenneth Starr in a yearlong crisis that transfixed the nation. With his Whitewater investigation stalled, Starr saw Clinton's sexual improprieties as a far more promising avenue, particularly after receiving Tripp's tapes, which seemed to

Linda Tripp (above) reads a statement to reporters on July 29, 1998. Following her eighth and final day of grand jury testimony, Tripp told the media, "I have been vilified for taking the path of truth."

At a 1994 press conference, Paula Jones (above) talks about her sexual harassment charges against President Clinton. Admitting no wrongdoing, Clinton agreed, in November 1998, to settle the case for $850,000.

catch Clinton in a lie: He had denied a sexual relationship with Lewinsky in a deposition he gave in the Paula Jones lawsuit. Starr's efforts, once devoted to weighty matters of political corruption, had now become reduced to investi-

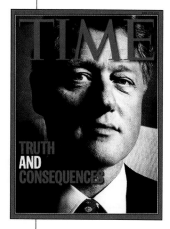

gating a philandering husband who lied about sex. A stained blue dress (belonging to Lewinsky) was confiscated for DNA testing. Secret-service officers, once an impenetrable buffer between the president and the outside world, were brought in for questioning. The president himself was forced to testify before a federal grand jury—via closed-circuit TV—and split hairs on the exact nature of his encounter with Lewinsky, admitting only to an "inappropriate" relationship with her. The 452-page Starr Report recounted in explicit detail the inquiry's findings and led the House

of Representatives to approve two articles of impeachment—for perjury and obstruction of justice (for allegedly assisting in the hiding of gifts to and from Lewinsky). Clinton thus became the second president, after Andrew Johnson in 1868, to be impeached. *Time* magazine *(inset)* summed up the damage Starr's duel with Clinton had done to the office of the president.

Americans clearly had no wish to see their president removed from office, particularly over a matter they perceived as purely personal and largely motivated by partisan malice. In the end there was little doubt that both articles of impeachment would fail to receive the

Clinton publicly denies having had sexual relations with Monica Lewinsky (above, right). The affair between Lewinsky and Clinton prompted a best-selling exposé written by Andrew Morton (inset, right).

Independent counsel Kenneth Starr is sworn in prior to presenting his report to the Judiciary Committee's impeachment inquiry on November 19, 1998.

MONICA'S STORY

ANDREW MORTON

Author of the #1 *New York Times* bestseller *Diana: Her True Story*

required two-thirds majority vote in the Senate. For some, the public's opposition to Clinton's removal was a sign of declining moral standards, for others it was simply a sign of good sense and perspective, two qualities often in short supply in Washington's overheated environment.

Bill Clinton had survived, but not unscathed. "However much he may pride himself on supernatural skills as an escape artist," wrote historian Arthur Schlesinger Jr., "he can never escape the stain of presidential misbehavior and personal betrayal."

The Hillary Factor

I suppose I could have stayed home and baked cookies and had teas," Hillary Rodham Clinton said during the 1992 presidential campaign. Instead, she became a law professor, a litigator, and a feminist. A "Buy One/Get One Free" campaign button promised a White House partnership, and, indeed, Hillary proved to be the president's most trusted adviser. She survived her ordeal as head of the ill-fated healthcare reform effort and went on to become a strong advocate for children and the author of *It Takes A Village,* a book on community responsibility in childrearing.

But her actions also stirred controversy. She was attacked for her role in dismissing White House travel aides and for allegedly hiding papers after the suicide of her former law partner, Vincent Foster. Subpoenaed in the Whitewater inquiry to explain missing records, she became the first president's wife to testify before a federal grand jury. When the Lewinsky scandal broke, she publicly blamed a "vast right-wing conspiracy" and privately suffered.

But the pain and embarrassment yielded a surprising dividend as her approval ratings skyrocketed in sympathy for the wronged wife who stood by her man. Buoyed by the support, Hillary Rodham Clinton made her own history by moving to New York and running for the Senate—the only first lady ever to seek elected office.

First Lady Hillary Rodham Clinton greets supporters (above) in Westchester, New York. In 1999 the first lady contemplated a run for the Senate; she formally announced her candidacy early in 2000.

In the midst of the Lewinsky scandal, the Clinton family, including First Dog Buddy, leave the White House together on their way to Camp David on July 24, 1998.

Pleasure Principles

★

LIFESTYLE TRENDS OF THE 90S

A t the start of the decade, it seemed that a sluggish economy would dovetail with a simpler approach to life—an antidote to the consumerism of the '80s. But the stock market boomed, the Internet took off, and the pace of life became turbocharged. Cell phones and laptop computers became ubiquitous in offices, airports, and pants pockets; aggressive SUVs abounded on the road; and fashion became as eclectic as the wild and sometimes weird World Wide Web itself. Even children suddenly got busy, spending hours poring over the latest Pokémon cards or frantically manipulating the joysticks connected to the latest video games. And with people working out and working long hours, no one had the time to eat right. Enter the PowerBar (*inset*) and grocery-bagfuls of fitness-oriented foods.

Along with the Internet culture came a loosening of attitudes that mirrored the freewheeling character of the online universe. Greater acceptance of lesbians and gay men became widespread, offices went casual, and millions of Americans took refuge in laid-back living room-style coffee bars. A time of personal freedom, nearly unlimited choices, and having it both ways, the '90s could be aptly summed up by the buzzword the decade generated: "whatever."

In-line skating (left) was a popular form of exercise and, in some cities, commuting. The U.S. National Sporting Goods Association estimated that by 1994 the country had more than 12 million in-line skaters.

The Thrill of Sports

A new breed of athletes—adrenaline junkies constantly on the lookout for novel, exciting, and often dangerous physical challenges—generated a subculture called "extreme sports" in the '90s. Some of the pursuits were like nothing sports enthusiasts had ever seen, but others—snowboarding, street luge, sky surfing, for example—were hybrids of established sports or variations tweaked for maximum thrill yield.

The extreme end of extreme sports, which included sky surfing (sky diving with a board strapped to the feet) and street luge (hurtling downhill at more than 70 miles per hour while lying flat on a roller sled without brakes), was generally viewed by the mainstream as the province of lunatics, not athletes. Snowboarding, mountain biking, and climbing, however, won large followings. The snowboard, after starting out as novelty snow-sports equipment in 1965, became the backbone of a burgeoning winter industry. By 1998, more than 5.5 million people had traded in their skis for the skateboarding/surfing-style ride of the snowboard. Climbers who couldn't get to the legendary rocks of Yosemite—or to Everest, which was so popular its base camps became crowded—scaled indoor artificial climbing walls.

Mountain bikers took their wheels through every terrain imaginable, including snow-covered peaks. Not content with the free fall of bungee jumping, air-addicted thrill seekers opted for the mostly illegal sport of BASE jumping—leaping off buildings or bridges with parachutes strapped to their backs (the acronym stood for buildings, antenna tower, span, earth).

In 1995 ESPN gave extreme sports a boost by creating and broadcasting the X Games, featuring extreme-sports athletes in summer and winter competitions. And snowboarding became an official Olympic sport at the 1998 Winter Games in Nagano.

An in-line skater at the '97 Summer X Games (above) takes some air (has both skates off the ground at the same time). At Stratton, Vermont, in 1996, a snowboarder (top) goes airborne in the half-pipe, a U-shaped ramp.

Rock climber Ron Kauk, who set standards for difficult climbing in the '70s, solos Yosemite's Killer Pillar in 1998 at age 40. The sport's popularity led to artificial climbing walls and the terms rock jock, wall rat, and hang dog.

New York City's annual gay-pride parade, the largest in the country, attracts friends and families of gays as well as young men determined to make a splash on one of the many floats. The man below rides 1997's Splash Bar float.

Gay Pride and Prejudice

O n balance, the gay community in the '90s made headway in its campaign for civil rights and acceptance by mainstream America. Pop culture saw the coming out of comedian Ellen DeGeneres and musicians Melissa Etheridge and K. D. Lang. The TV sitcom *Will & Grace* featured a gay main character. Corporations from Disney to Xerox extended benefits to same-sex domestic partners, and 11 states banned discrimination against homosexuals. The Internet gave closeted homosexuals and those living in rural

---

"The acceptance of homosexuality is the last step in the decline of Gentile civilization."

Pat Robertson, of the Christian Broadcasting Network

---

areas access to a larger community. Gay-pride parades attracted diverse participants, including uniformed gay police officers and "Dykes on Bikes." An estimated 750,000 marched on Washington for gay rights in 1993. And when Bill Clinton was inaugurated, pride and hope ran high—during his campaign, he had told the gay community, "I have a vision for America and you're part of it."

Clinton vowed to secure homosexuals fair and equal treatment in the military and to wage war on AIDS. Though he failed on the first count, after 21-year-old Matthew Shepard was viciously murdered in Wyoming simply for being gay, Clinton did urge lawmakers to broaden existing hate-crime laws to include acts against homosexuals. The Supreme Court also came to the defense of gay Americans by overturning Colorado's Amendment Two, which would have denied homosexuals their civil rights.

But the growing visibility of gays also mobilized the religious right— the group ran TV ads insisting that gays could be "cured." And despite his promises, Clinton signed the Defense of Marriage Act in 1996, which allowed states to disregard same-sex marriages performed in another state and denied federal benefits to gay couples who marry.

Comedian Ellen DeGeneres (left) and actress Anne Heche make a public statement about their private lives. DeGeneres came out twice—in real life and in an episode of her TV sitcom, Ellen.

Toys Rule

Though the new generation of toys that arrived in the '90s did not push perennial favorites Barbie, Lego, and Play-Doh off shelves, they did claim prime aisle space in stores. Top sellers included three endowed with a microchip: cuddly *Sesame Street* character Tickle Me Elmo, gibberish-talking Furby, and "virtual" pet Tamagotchi. Dominating the decade, though, were Beanie Babies—small beanbag animals with names like Humphrey the camel and Quackers the duck that were produced in limited series. Beanie Babies became a collectible sensation, earning $250 million by 1999.

Rivaling the Beanie Babies craze was Pokémon (short for "pocket monsters"), a series of toys—trading cards, key chains, miniature figures, a cartoon show—based on an electronic game from Japan. The mania surrounding the toys reached such a pitch that many schools across the country banned them.

The decade brought a trend in which almost half of all toys were linked to a movie, a TV show, a book, and/or music. Snapping up Power Rangers, Teenage Mutant Ninja Turtles, and *Toy Story* dolls, to name a few marketing crossovers, Americans bought an estimated $22.5 billion worth of toys in 1999.

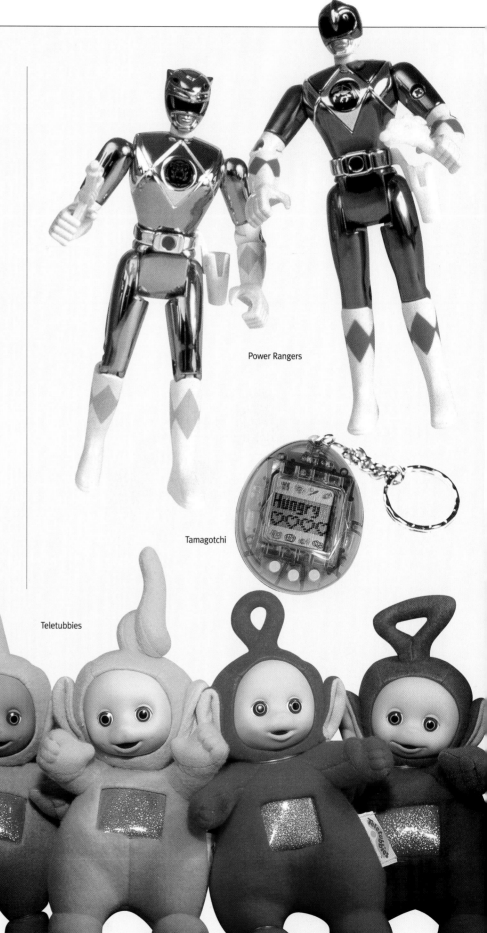

Power Rangers

Tamagotchi

Teletubbies

Ninja Turtle

Furby

Stores had to rush to keep their supply of Pokémon trading cards (left), which were based on the video game, up with demand. In the few weeks before Christmas 1999, Pokémon generated nearly $5 billion in revenues and was not yet at the peak of its popularity.

Beanie Babies

Pokémon

Basic Pokémon
Pikachu
40 HP

Mouse Pokémon. Length: 1' 4", Weight: 13 lbs.

Gnaw   10

Thunder Jolt Flip a coin. If
tails, Pikachu does 10 damage
to itself.   30

weakness   resistance   retreat cost

When several of these Pokémon gather, their electricity can
cause lightning storms. LV. 12 #25

It's All in the Game

With a growth rate twice that of the movie business, and annual revenues of $6.3 billion, the electronic-games industry in the 1990s was poised to eclipse Hollywood in both dollars and cultural impact. The days of video-arcade games like Pong, Pac-Man, and Space Invaders were long gone. And although console-based games from Nintendo, Sega, and PlayStation became faster and more sophisticated, the real force behind the industry's explosive growth came from personal-computer games.

Adults tended to choose task-oriented titles—such as Civilization and SimCity, in which civilizations and cities were created and then managed—but also spent countless hours at bat, behind the wheel, and passing from the pocket in simulated sports games. The 1993 adventure game Myst became the best-selling PC game of all time. By the end of the decade, though, its beautifully rendered images seemed outmoded.

Video-game competition started young (opposite) in many families. Myst (left) challenges players to solve the disappearance of a team of scientists. Video games, played with a console (bottom left) or hand-held device (bottom), faced increasing competition from computer-based games like Myst, Doom, and Quake.

"[The games' increasing realism] makes people think they can shoot someone and it doesn't hurt."

Eugene Provenzo, professor, University of Miami, and critic of violent computer games

The introduction of even more advanced graphics gave gamers the illusion of tremendous speed and unlimited maneuverability. Complex and gory shoot-'em-up games such as Doom and Quake required 60 to 80 hours to play. Their cutting-edge technology administered such powerful doses of virtual violence that some politicians, psychologists, and parents held the games accountable for a terrifying spate of shootings involving young people, claiming the games had desensitized the killers to the consequences of extreme violence. Infamous teenage murderers in Paducah, Kentucky, and Littleton, Colorado, were later found to be avid players of such games.

Of course, not all Doom players were prone to violence, and the majority of games were not violent in nature at all. But there was no doubt that graphic technology in the '90s had reached a level where, for some players, computer games were no longer an escape from reality, but a barrier to it.

Office Politics

People so identified with the comic strip Dilbert, about life in the cubicle ranks, that the character (center) got his own television show and a trip to the New York Stock Exchange to promote it. Pictured at the bell-ringing event are (from left) Richard Grasso, chairman of the stock exchange, Douglas Stern, president and CEO of United Media, and William Burleigh, president and CEO of E. W. Scripps Company.

A mother's work is never done—especially when she has a laptop computer and a job that requires commuting by air. In Boston, one of the new airport commuters (above) uses e-mail to dispense motherly advice and keep tabs on her children.

American workplaces changed dramatically in the 1990s. Younger men, more women, and minorities of all ages were reaching the upper echelons of corporations and competing with graying white male executives for top positions. Seemingly secure workers found themselves downsized in the early '90s and struggled to build "portable skills." Young entrepreneurs revolutionized the way companies did business (using the Internet) and the workplace itself. The 40-hour week was abandoned for the "90-hours-a-week-and-loving-it" sentiment that Apple Computer made fashionable in the 1980s. Accordingly, employees at new-economy pioneers like Yahoo! and Excite shed suits and worked in shorts, T-shirts, and sandals. In corporate America, the less radical concept of "dressing down" on Fridays began to spread and quickly became known as "casual Friday." Soon, 75 percent of the Fortune 500 companies allowed casual dress—what came to be called "business casual"—at least one day per week; the hope was that more comfortable dress would boost productivity and morale.

The concern about morale stemmed from the growing numbers of unhappy workers confined to cramped cubicles under increasingly out-of-touch managers. Such conditions were the subject of the comic strip *Dilbert*. Drawn by former Pacific Bell employee Scott Adams, it featured the geeky Dilbert—a mouthless, down-trodden cubicle dweller with a permanently crooked tie—in all-too-realistic office situations.

In the spring of 1999, Jane Slade (center) heads Amazon.com's customer-service department. The division's cramped layout epitomized

Out of Fashion

The '90s saw an almost total shift away from the flashy and corporate looks of the '80s to more informal attire. The institution of casual Fridays at the office was the first sign of a sartorial sea change. And though there was a resurgence of '70s-style looks—halter tops, bell-bottoms, platform shoes, and psychedelic patterns—that only the young and thinnest could wear, most of what was considered fashionable had a wide appeal. Chains like the GAP and Eileen Fisher offered comfortable, neat, and moderately stylish clothes to millions.

> "In the '80s it was so incredibly over the top. Now it's about how we can express ourselves and still maintain a certain amount of dignity."
>
> Isaac Mizrahi, New York City designer, on '90s fashion

Tired of '80s fads, American women had begun "shopping in their own closets" (industry parlance for not shopping at all), provoking Donna Karan, Ralph Lauren, Calvin Klein, and other designers to create clothes that were simple, elegant, and wearable. The result, "casual luxe," allowed women to move easily from work to play. Beaded tank tops or cashmere sweater sets coupled with A-line skirts of silk or leather reintroduced classic glamour into many wardrobes.

The '90s was also the decade that let underwear out of the closet. Catalog giant Victoria's Secret opened up the world of lingerie to a receptive general audience in malls across America. The Wonderbra, in particular, fed a sudden, cross-generational demand for enhanced cleavage.

Generation Xers—the label attached to upstart men and women in their 20s—immersed themselves in retro fashion: denim outfits, polyester shirts and pants, ethnic creations. Xers also embraced grunge, a lifestyle statement that included torn jeans, flannel shirts, knit caps, and body piercing.

Actress Lisa Kudrow (right) attends the 71st Academy Awards in a wearable ensemble that typifies '90s elegance. A casual shirt and khakis (above) became appropriate office and weekend attire.

Thrift shops and surplus stores inspired '90s youth. They mixed—never matched—their clothes, and were partial to heavy shoes and hair that was sculpted or somehow askew.

Skin Deep

As the hard-edged punk look of the '80s gave way to the frayed grunge look of the '90s, teens and young adults turned to body art for self-expression. They lined up and waited to take their markings, and soon people became accustomed to the sight of a metal ball or ring accenting a chin, eyebrow, nose, bellybutton, or tongue. Tattoos, once associated with the taut biceps of a sailor, were now prevalent on both sexes and included lovers' names, cartoon faces, thorny armbands, and Chinese characters. Whether they were motivated by the desire to buck unrealistic beauty standards in a celebrity-obsessed culture or to make parents cringe, droves of young adults put their bodies in the hands of piercers and tattoo artists who often had no medical training or certification for their trade.

A Matter of Taste *Despite warnings of possible infection and chipped teeth, many fearlessly studded their tongues.*

Drawing the Line *As of 1999, 30 states had enacted laws prohibiting minors from getting tattoos, and 19 passed laws against piercing minors.*

Fat Free, but Getting Fatter

America's war on fat, part of the fitness craze that began in the '80s, matured into a multibillion-dollar industry in the next decade. Low-fat, no-fat, and "lite" cheeses, salad dressing, ice cream, cookies, and chips, to name a few of the altered foods, descended on grocery stores. But many were of dubious nutritional value, and certainly not calorie free. The most controversial ingredient in low-fat snack foods was Olestra, a fat substitute that passes through the digestive system without being absorbed, thus leaving no fat behind. Fat paranoia fueled an interest in ethnic foods—such as sushi, some Mexican and Indian dishes, vegetarian pizzas and pasta—that were naturally low in fat.

Thousands of Americans entered the Zone, a protein-based, anticarbohydrate diet crafted by Dr. Barry Sears. But if giving up bread and pasta was hard, losing weight, for many, was nearly impossible. Despite a national campaign to raise awareness about the dangers of being overweight (it can lead to hypertension, heart disease, and diabetes), about 35 percent of the population needed to lose weight at the end of the decade. McDonald's underscored the country's weakness when it dropped its low-fat McLean hamburger after sluggish sales and replaced it with the fat-saturated Arch Deluxe.

Couscous

Indian food

Mexican food

Sushi platter

Cookies

Potato chips

Soup

Salad dressing

Less really does turn out to be more. Chips, cookies, and other fat-free packaged foods gave many Americans an excuse to binge. George Foreman (top right) entered the nutrition ring with his grease-eliminating Foreman Grill.

Crazy for Coffee

During a decade in which speed was paramount, coffee emerged as the national elixir. Not the standard "cuppa joe" variety—that sludgy, muddy-tasting stuff that sat thickening on diner warmers—but the arabica bean–connoisseur's beverage that came in multiple forms and required a phrase book just to order: "double decaf tall skinny latte with no foam," for example.

Once the province of students, poets, and aspiring musicians with more time than money, the country's roughly 700 laid-back coffeehouses suddenly multiplied into 10,000 decidedly caffeinated emporiums where the price of the average beverage equaled a half-hour of minimum-wage work. The days of the bottomless cup had vanished, but now coffee customers could linger, at least for a moment, and read newspapers or simply marvel at the velvety texture of the foam atop their cappuccinos.

Cafés in megabookstores like Borders and Barnes & Noble gave browsers a place to read entire chapters. In cyber cafés, where the '90s cults of technology and the bean merged, patrons nursed their concoctions while surfing the Net. And on popular TV shows like *Frasier* and *Friends* characters gathered to trade one-liners in coffeehouses. As final proof of America's evolved palate, 7-Eleven, Denny's, Dunkin' Donuts, and McDonald's all offered specialty brews.

Led by the publicly traded Starbucks chain, coffee bars nationwide attracted a steady stream of bleary-eyed commuters, techies, and students with cell phones and laptops in search of the quality java jolts listed below.

Caffè Latte Espresso and steamed milk, touched with foam

Cappuccino Espresso generously topped with foamed milk

Caffè Mocha Espresso, cocoa, steamed milk, and whipped cream

Mocha Valencia Valencia orange Caffe Mocha and added espresso

Caffè Americano Espresso's character, brewed coffee's strength

Caramel Macchiato Foamed milk with espresso, vanilla, and real caramel

Espresso Macchiato Espresso gently marked with foam

Espresso Con Panna Espresso topped with whipped cream

Iced Caffè Latte Espresso and milk over ice

By mid-decade, coffee was the second most traded commodity in the world; oil was first. Many New Yorkers bought theirs at Zabar's (above). The craze was enough to give Seattle, the country's gourmet-coffee capital, the Jitters, a drive-thru espresso joint (left).

"When is this story going to end?"

Mitch Speiser, financial analyst who followed Starbucks for Lehman Brothers in New York in 1998, on the coffee craze

America Gives Back

By the end of the '90s, Americans were more environmentally aware than ever before. Nine thousand communities—equal to half the U.S. population—had learned to sort garbage for paper, glass, cans, and compostables. Dedicated recyclers from Portland to Palm Beach dragged large colored bins to the ends of their driveways on curbside pickup day. Train commuters dutifully deposited newspapers in specially designed platform receptacles earmarked for recycling.

Often more expensive than merely dumping unsorted trash, recycling was nonetheless preferable to the nightmarish specter of overflowing landfills and pollutant-spewing incinerators. In an increasing number of states, individuals and businesses had no choice but to recycle. Enacted in 1990, California's Integrated Solid Waste Management Act, for example, demanded that each city reduce waste by 25 percent by 1995 and 50 percent by 2000. Similar measures were passed across the country. And by 1997 some 49 million tons of refuse churned through the recycling and composting infrastructure—a vast improvement over the eight million tons processed in 1970.

When public pressure in 1990 forced McDonald's, a notorious user of ozone-destroying polystyrene (Styrofoam) packaging, to adopt biodegradable paper boxes to keep burgers warm, it kick-started a trend in corporate accountability. Recycling became a marketing byword. Clothing, greeting cards, park benches, even toilet paper, touted eco-friendly origins. But as more and more package labels proclaimed the "organic" or recycled nature of their contents, American consumers—three-fourths of whom considered themselves environmentalists—had to be more careful than ever not to be "green-washed" by untrue claims.

Take It to the Curb

While rinsing plastic became habit, the process of recycling plastic remained in its infancy. The different types (below) could not all be recycled. PETE, HDPE, and V were widely recycled, LDPE less so, and PP was not recyclable at all.

Polyethylene Terephthalate (PETE): Soft-drink and water containers, some waterproof packaging.

High-Density Polyethylene (HDPE): Milk, detergent, and oil bottles; toys and plastic bags.

Vinyl/Polyvinyl Chloride (V): Food wrap, cooking-oil bottles, blister packages.

Low-Density Polyethylene (LDPE): Many different kinds of plastic bags, shrink wrap, garment bags.

Polypropylene (PP): Refrigerated containers, some bags, most bottle tops, some carpets, some food wrap.

Environmental groups calling for a ban on Styrofoam food packaging march in front of a San Diego McDonald's (opposite). The chain began phasing out the plastic in November 1990.

Evolution of the SUV Revolution

In the Beginning Among the SUVs vying for the attention of car buyers was Chevrolet's Blazer *(above, the 1994 model)*. Families were attracted to its four doors (the bare-bones Jeep had only two) and ample storage space. In '94 it sold for around $17,000.

Bigger Fares Better To replace its rugged, no-frills Bronco, Ford introduced the Expedition in 1997. One of the first "full-size" SUVs, it held nine people (smaller SUVs like Jeep Cherokee held six) and could tow 8,000 pounds. In '97 more than 200,000 were sold for around $30,000.

Luxury Takes Over By 1999 size wasn't enough, and designer SUVs owned the roads—or at least the parking lots at high-end malls. Mercedes *(above)* and BMW were among the luxury automakers that entered the SUV market. Fully equipped, these SUVs could cost over $50,000.

On the Road

Bumpy ride, poor gas mileage, and stiff, unresponsive handling hardly added up to a sound automotive purchase, particularly with sticker prices ranging from $17,000 in 1990 to more than $40,000 in 1999. Yet Americans snatched up sport-utility vehicles (SUVs) faster than dealers could stock them. Once a lowly military workhorse, the four-wheel-drive vehicle was suddenly the darling of showroom floors and three-car garages. The fact that most Cherokees, Pathfinders, and Explorers would never haul or tow anything mattered little, as did the estimate that fewer than 5 percent of SUVs on the road at the end of the decade would ever put their off-road capabilities to the test.

The bulky conveyance edged-out station wagons and minivans as the family vehicle of choice, and sales during the decade tripled—from one million in 1990 to 3.1 million in 1999. And by mid-decade, SUVs with buttery leather interiors and top-of-the-line sound systems had supplanted pricey foreign sedans in driveways across the country. Rather than lose market share, luxury automakers Mercedes, Lexus, BMW, and Lincoln all introduced a version of the SUV.

Despite their popularity, SUVs did have detractors. The high-riding behemoths (especially those with tinted windows) obstructed the views of drivers in cars. Their overpowered engines guzzled gas and caused more air pollution than standard cars. And in collisions with lower-riding sedans and wagons, they proved extremely dangerous. Why urbanites and suburban retirees required an SUV to fetch a latte was anyone's guess. Still, they proliferated—even on the streets of Manhattan.

And as they grew in popularity, they grew in size. In the late '90s, Ford and Chevrolet unveiled even longer, taller, and wider SUVs. Fortunately by 1999 President Clinton had responded to environmental concerns by announcing that light trucks and SUVs would be subject to the same pollution-control standards as passenger cars.

With its pickups, vans, and SUVs, Route 22 in Allentown, Pennsylvania, could be any road in '90s America. Though SUVs neither rode nor handled like passenger cars, they often replaced them.

Wired Nation

★

LIFE ON THE INFORMATION SUPERHIGHWAY

With each passing year, computers processed more and more information at faster speeds. Terms not used the previous decade—words like *Internet*, *browser*, *online*, and *e-mail*—were common by 1995. And with the help of satellite dishes (*below*), information technology, once limited to the office, moved into the home and onto the street, opening up trillions of miles of information pathways and creating hundreds of personal-communications gadgets. People expected computers to do more, and they expected to be able to access the information computers stored anytime and from anywhere. The combination of more affordable hardware and user-friendly software fueled the market for home computers. In 1990, 25.4 percent of American households had access to a personal computer; by 1999, almost 60 percent did, with many people using the computers available at public libraries, "cyber cafes," and other retail businesses. Due to the introduction of electronic mail into the mainstream, the number of Americans working at home for an employer grew to 20 million in 1999. People also began using e-mail to establish and maintain personal relationships. Whether using their computers for personal or business purposes, Americans tapped into a worldwide network of information known as the World Wide Web.

The late-'90s Apple iMac (left) promised user-friendly operations, fast connection to the Internet, and a fun, colorful computer experience.

Work by Tim Berners-Lee in the early '90s led to the creation of the World Wide Web. As a boy, Berners-Lee built his first computer from a television set and spare parts.

Global Reach

The vast reach, popularity, and economic impact of the World Wide Web belied its rather recent beginnings as a research tool for academics in the 1980s. Tim Berners-Lee, a software developer for the European Particle Physics Laboratory in Geneva, Switzerland, created the basis for the Web in 1983 when he solved the problem of how to collect and link information stored on computers scattered around the globe.

Berners-Lee began working with a communications network called the Advanced Research Projects Agency Network developed by the Defense Department in 1969 using cables and telephone wires. He applied the new technologies for encoding and linking documents and experimented with universal resource locators (URLs), which effectively gave documents their own addresses. This made it possible for anyone who knew the system to retrieve information stored on other computers. Envisioning a humanistic tool for cross-cultural communication, Berners-Lee persuaded the laboratory to release the network—a vast web of connections—to the public, which it did in April 1992. The race to map, and make money from, the ever-expanding "internet" was on.

Point-and-click computer graphics adapted by Marc Andreessen (above) simplified Web browsing. Within a year of founding Netscape more than two million copies of the firm's browser had been downloaded.

> "If [computer networking] were a traditional science, Berners-Lee would win a Nobel Prize."
>
> Eric Schmidt, Novell CEO, *Time,* March 29, 1999

By early 1993, researchers at the University of Illinois had created Mosaic, a user-friendly World Wide Web browser. Mosaic allowed computer users to navigate the Web by typing an address on-screen. These addresses became known as Web sites, and they led to the creation of more browsers. The entrepreneurs behind these browsers—Marc Andreessen and Jim Clark of Netscape (previously Mosaic), Steve Case of America Online, and Bill Gates of Microsoft and its Internet Explorer—became some of the decade's most well-known and influential figures. While providing access to the Internet, they ensured the success of their medium: By 1998, 102 million people worldwide could visit some 1.8 million Web sites.

Millions of Americans navigated the Web and sent e-mail with greater ease thanks to Steve Case (above), CEO of America Online. In 1998, more than half the country's Internet users logged on through AOL.

> "Our vision is to build a place to find and discover anything our customers might want to buy."
>
> Amazon's Jeff Bezos, *Time,* December

Time names Jeff Bezos, CEO of Amazon.com, its 1999 Person of the Year (above). Bezos turned his bookselling site into a retailing business that hawked everything from electronics to lawn chairs. It attracted eight million visitors per month.

Not Your Average Millionaire

With its power to attract millions of people, the Internet quickly became an arena in which to make millions of dollars. By the end of the '90s, young, risk-hungry entrepreneurs had turned what was once simply information-sharing technology into a vast cyber marketplace open around the clock. How to exchange goods and services through the Internet seemed to be on everyone's mind. And market-savvy Americans who didn't own an Internet company or work for one bought stock in a business that was linked to the Web.

Toward the end of the decade, the stock market was driven to all-time highs partly due to the rush to own shares in Internet-related companies. Even though most Internet ventures had yet to show a profit, their stocks, which were growing exponentially in price, attracted buyers. Infusions of venture capital enabled marginally profitable Internet operations—which quickly earned the nickname "dot-coms," after the period ("dot") and domain name ("com") in their Web addresses—to masquerade as sound businesses and their owners to become millionaires, at least on paper.

Most of the new generation of business tycoons were self-made and from the middle class, and cared little about appearances—their own or their offices'. They cared about technology, though (it was fun!), and spent most of their time tweaking it. David Filo and Jerry Yang, for example, created the search engine Yahoo!, the most widely used site on the Web, while graduate students at Stanford: In 1994, they started organizing their favorite Web sites and found there was a huge demand for the service. By 1998, each was worth more than a billion dollars.

Meg Whitman, CEO of eBay, an online auction house, became the first female Internet billionaire when she exercised an option to buy 7.2 million shares from the company in 1998. Launched in 1995, eBay was one of only a few e-businesses to be solvent from its inception. The risk of debt didn't deter Jeff Bezos, founder of the online bookseller Amazon.com, from pursuing his dream to create the earth's biggest store. Although his company had yet to turn a profit at the close of the decade, Amazon.com's public stock offering in 1997 made Bezos a billionaire.

Meg Whitman (above), CEO of eBay, the nation's most successful online auction house, helped create a forum for consumers to use e-mail to buy and sell items ranging from cars to flatware. In 1998, some six million people found a reason to visit the eBay auction house each month. The most popular items that year: baseball cards, Beanie Babies stuffed animals, and antiques.

Jerry Yang (left) created the Web search engine Yahoo! with fellow graduate student David Filo. They picked the name because it was "irreverent" and "reflective of the Wild West nature of the Internet," said Yang. Their initial investor said he would take back his million dollars if they changed it.

Connect the Dots

Technology prophets had long predicted that computers would one day be as integral to the home as the telephone. But it wasn't until the Internet burst on the scene that their predictions began to come true. By 1994, Americans were spending as much on personal computers as they were on televisions, and by the end of the decade, Americans were using their computers to shop for (*right, from top*) airline tickets (priceline.com), groceries (ShopRite.com), medications (duanereade.com), books (amazon.com), and other goods; to seek medical and financial advice; to get their news (CNN.com, *bottom*); and to perform many other essential functions. Students used browsers like Yahoo! (*opposite, top left*) to get help with their homework. People bought clothes from Lands' End (*opposite, bottom*) and other retailers, purchased cars and houses, and ordered expensive jewelry from Tiffany & Co. (*opposite, right*). They rented apartments by going online. They listened to music using the Web and visited the Web sites of movies about to be released.

In cyber chat rooms—sites that allowed users to communicate with others online—people could flirt anonymously or give or seek advice. In some cases, lasting relationships, even marriages, resulted.

And by the 1999 presidential primaries, every candidate had a Web site and campaigned on the Internet.

Twenty-six-year-old DotComGuy (above), formerly Mitch Maddox, attempted to live off e-commerce from home for a year. Maddox, who spent much of the '90s preparing for the experiment that began in January 2000, and for which he legally changed his name, ordered food and clothes online and hosted a 24-hour video of his life.

The new Apple iMac (above) promised user-friendly operations, fast connection to the Internet, and a fun, colorful computer experience to which children especially took.

Gotta Get a Gadget

Initially, it was about necessity. Hospitals needed to be able to reach doctors and traveling salespeople needed to be accessible to their clients and bosses and colleagues. Pagers were among the first personal-communications devices to catch on in the '90s, but by the end of the decade an array of electronic communications gadgets—cellular phones, laptop computers, personal digital assistants—had joined pagers as favorite communications tools. Using them had become a habit, and they were almost as common as a purse or wallet.

The cellular phone was an anomaly in the '80s, but by 1999, 70 million people in the United States alone had cell-phone service. Moms at soccer games, commuters on buses

> ## "I feel like I have Batman's utility belt on. All I need is a Batarang and a spool of Batcable."
>
> Dan Hoyer, avid owner of electronic gadgets

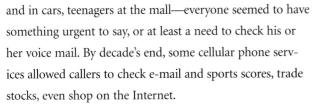

Tools—or toys—linked to the communications craze: personal digital assistant (left) and digital camera (below). Cell phones (bottom) and pagers (below) allowed people to connect round the clock from almost anywhere on an ever-smaller planet. These could connect to desktop computers to share pictures and information.

and in cars, teenagers at the mall—everyone seemed to have something urgent to say, or at least a need to check his or her voice mail. By decade's end, some cellular phone services allowed callers to check e-mail and sports scores, trade stocks, even shop on the Internet.

The laptop computer, another electronic device that became hugely popular, made it possible for people to work almost anywhere. Manufacturers took the power of a desktop computer and packaged it in a portable, book-sized device that transformed trains, hotel rooms, and airports into work stations. Laptop owners could also watch a movie on the devices's built-in DVD player or play a game on its CD-ROM drive.

Compared with personal digital assistants (PDAs), such as Palm Pilots, which came on the scene in 1992,

laptops looked almost as bulky as desktop computers. Slightly larger than a deck of cards, a PDA could keep track of appointments, phone numbers, and to-do lists, and perform e-mail functions. PDAs also were compatible with most personal computers and office software.

By the end of the '90s, manufacturers were planning a "supergadget" that would combine the functions of a PDA with those of a cellular phone, which meant users could look forward to a device that would allow them to be more efficient and productive than ever.

Microsoft's Bill Gates announces the new Windows 95 program (named for its year of introduction, 1995) at a press conference in Redmond, Washington. The Tonight Show's Jay Leno was on hand and the Rolling Stones' "Start Me Up" blared in the background. The decade saw Gates become the richest man in America.

Public Hero, or Public Enemy?

Perhaps no other technology company had as much impact on the '90s as Microsoft, the software company founded by Bill Gates, a Harvard dropout, and his friend Paul Allen in 1975. Microsoft's Windows operating system and Office software (*bottom right*), known for their user-friendliness, lit up computer screens in offices, homes, and schools, practically guaranteeing a volatile relationship between Microsoft and others in the technology field.

Financially, Microsoft soared in the '90s. Soon after the May 1990 release of Windows 3.0, the company's updated operating system, sales hit $1.18 billion, and in 1999, the company employed 32,000 people in 60 countries. By 1993, 25 million PCs ran on Windows, and in 1992 alone, 39 percent of all personal-computer applications sold were for Windows. Success brought scrutiny, however, and in 1993 the Justice Department launched an investigation into Microsoft's business practices. The central issue was Microsoft's linking its Internet browser, Explorer, with its operating system, potentially depriving Windows users of a choice of browsers. Rival companies, 20 states, and the Justice Department argued before Judge Thomas Penfield Jackson that the tactic was anticompetitive, and in 2000 the court agreed. Gates accused the courts of stifling innovation. Critics countered that a software industry not dominated by Microsoft is the best environment in which to innovate. Legal troubles did not prevent Microsoft from earning $19.7 billion in 1999, though by 2000 the company's stock had fallen considerably.

District court judge Thomas Penfield Jackson (above) found that Microsoft illegally squelched competition by including its Explorer Web browser in its PC operating system. Jackson's Findings of Fact in the antitrust case is at left.

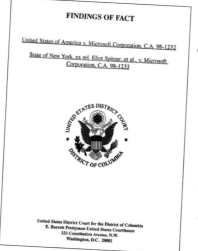

"It was Microsoft—not the government—that has suppressed innovation."

Eliot Spitzer, New York State attorney general, responding to Bill Gates's assertion that Microsoft was wrongly accused of monopolistic behavior

Flushed with Victory

★

A GOLDEN AGE FOR SPORTS

Sports figures loomed large during the 1990s. In a survey conducted late in the decade, the Associated Press asked urban children to name the two figures they admired most: The result was a tie, between God and—Michael Jordan. Jordan, who led the Chicago Bulls to six National Basketball Association titles in the '90s, certainly played divinely: Who could imagine there would be an athlete to rival him? But then along came Tiger Woods, the prodigiously talented, multiracial superstar from Stanford, who took the PGA by storm in his rookie season of 1996, then proceeded to dominate the golfing terrain like no one since Jack Nicklaus. Like Jordan, Woods had what the country demanded of its greatest athletes: He was talented and telegenic, and had worldwide, corporate appeal.

Due to history-making performances by a wide range of athletes, almost every sport was in the spotlight. The U.S. gave figure skating its youngest Olympic gold medal winner ever; the NBA launched a successful sister league, the WNBA; and the U.S. won the 1999 Women's World Cup soccer tournament. Olympic runners and speed skaters broke world records, and tennis, thanks to its newest players, displayed a new kind of athleticism. Baseball saw several athletes pursue some of the game's most hallowed records. A baseball signed and dated by Mark McGwire *(inset)* testifies to his record-breaking 62nd single-season home run.

At age 21, Tiger Woods (left) became the youngest player ever to win the Masters, by a record 12 strokes. Fellow golfer Peter Jacobsen put it simply: "He's the greatest player in the history of the game."

Michael Jordan flies to the hoop against the New York Knicks in Madison Square Garden, the site of several of his most prolific scoring explosions.

Dynasty in Chicago

The Chicago Bulls dominated the National Basketball Association in the 1990s as no team had done since the vaunted Boston Celtics of Bill Russell in the 1950s and '60s. To win six titles in a decade would be remarkable in any age, but to do so in the modern era of free agency, with many players changing teams on a virtually annual basis, made the Bulls' feat nothing less than spectacular. Much of the credit must go to the mighty Michael Jordan, who transformed a perennial loser into one of sports' most feared dynasties. But others deserve mention as well: the mercurial Scottie Pippen, he of the swooping drives to the basket and the tenacious defense; Dennis Rodman, one of sports' most entertaining flakes but a demon rebounder; and, of course, the ringmaster who held it all together, coach Phil Jackson.

Getting to the top was no cakewalk. Though Jordan's raw talent propelled the Bulls to the playoffs in his rookie season of 1984–85, it would be six years before his team was able to win a championship by unseating Magic Johnson's Los Angeles Lakers in 1991. Things got easier after that, as Jordan matured into the finest player the game has ever seen and a shifting constellation of teammates happily settled in as invaluable role players. Harvey Grant, Steve Kerr, B. J. Armstrong—these are just a few of the supporting players who helped Jordan achieve his amazing pair of threepeats in 1991, '92, '93 and 1996, '97, '98. The Chicago juggernaut might well have won eight in a row had not Jordan, apparently looking for a new challenge, left the game for nearly two seasons to try his hand at baseball, an unsuccessful experiment that he wisely terminated. In the end, he went out in classic Jordan style, stealing the ball from Utah's Karl Malone and sinking the jumper that clinched a sixth title for Chicago. At 35, Jordan decided to retire—this time for good. Superman had left the building.

After three years of failure in the play-offs, an exhausted but proud Michael Jordan hugs the 1991 NBA Championship Trophy, the first of six he would bring home to Chicago.

Michael Jordan celebrates the Bulls' 1997 NBA title, their fifth, with teammates Scottie Pippen (below left) and Dennis Rodman (right).

A view from behind Houston catcher Brad Ausmus shows the powerful swing that the Cardinals' Mark McGwire used to blast a record 70 home runs in 1998.

Streaks and Strikes

Baseballs flew out of ballparks like popcorn from a lidless pot, as stronger hitters, smaller fields, and a shrinking strike zone made pitching seem a lost art. Thirty home runs in a season, once the benchmark of a slugger, became commonplace. In 1998 fans packed stadiums in record numbers to watch St. Louis's Mark McGwire and Chicago's Sammy Sosa chase Roger Maris's decades-old single-season home run record of 61. McGwire, with 70, broke the record first; Sosa hit 66.

But baseball had suffered through its share of growing pains, too. The financial disparity between large-market and small-market franchises continued to grow, and when the owners tried to impose a salary cap to encourage competitive balance, the players went on strike. The ensuing stalemate led to the cancellation of the 1994 World Series and alienated millions of fans.

Baltimore's blue-collar champion, Cal Ripken Jr., helped to lure them back in '95 with his stirring pursuit of Lou Gehrig's 56-year-old record of consecutive games played. The feel-good story reached a climax on September 6 as Ripken, playing before an ecstatic crowd in Baltimore's Camden Yards, broke Gehrig's mark by appearing in his 2,131st consecutive game.

Gehrig's descendants, the New York Yankees, reestablished themselves as baseball's great dynasty, winning the World Series in 1996, '98, and '99.

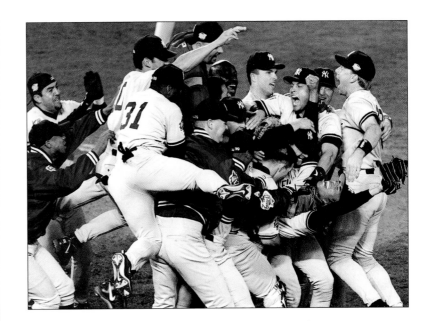

The 1998 New York Yankees celebrate their 24th World Series victory, a record. The team won an American League record of 114 regular-season games and outscored opponents by 309 runs, then blew through the play-offs and swept the San Diego Padres for the title.

Cal Ripken Jr., shakes hands with fans after breaking Lou Gehrig's record for consecutive games played. "Sports for me has always been a combination of love and persistence," Ripken has said. "That's who I am, how I approach things. I was brought up a certain way. If I wanted to play, and I could play, then I would. With no questions asked." Through it all, Ripken retained his focus: "My obligation is to myself and my team and how I approach the game, not to the streak."

A Woman's World

When Brandi Chastain buried her crucial penalty kick and famously shed her jersey in celebration at the 1999 Women's World Cup (WWC), she became a triumphant, high-profile symbol of the success of Title IX legislation. But the 1974 ruling, which mandated equal funding and opportunity for women's sports, had been paying dividends for years, producing a generation of brilliant female athletes in the U.S. who proved once and for all that running, kicking, or throwing "like a girl" was no longer a schoolyard insult.

Chastain was only the latest—and most visible—in a long line. The U.S. women's soccer team, Title IX beneficiaries all, had won the first WWC in 1991, and at the '96 Olympic Games in Atlanta, U.S. women won a gold medal in team gymnastics for the first time. American women won 18 other gold medals that summer, including the inaugural golds in softball and soccer. In 1997, the Women's National Basketball Association debuted to much fanfare, and at the Winter Olympics at Nagano in '98, the U.S. women's hockey team defeated Canada for the gold.

But none of these events received the media coverage that the '99 WWC did. The final between the U.S. and China at the Rose Bowl drew more than 90,000 spectators (the largest crowd ever to witness a women's sporting event), with millions more watching on television. During the tournament American striker Mia Hamm briefly became the most recognized female athlete in the world, sharing top billing with Michael Jordan in a series of sports drink commercials. The team went on to appear on magazine covers, on the front pages of newspapers, and on talk shows. Chastain's iconic, title-clinching pose (*left*) was everywhere, boldly announcing to the world that women athletes could keep up with the boys.

Brandi Chastain, known to teammates as "Hollywood," celebrates winning the 1999 Women's World Cup at the Rose Bowl. "Brandi wanted this more than anyone, and she knew what to do with it," said teammate Kate Sobrero.

Cynthia Cooper, of the Houston Comets, drives against the New York Liberty in 1997. That year, the WNBA's first, Cooper led the league in scoring with 22.2 points per game and spurred the Comets to the first of four consecutive league championships.

Dark Moments

In Germany, officials tend to Monica Seles immediately after a fan of rival Steffi Graf stabbed her in the back in 1993. Seles did not return to competitive tennis until more than two years later.

> "His life seemed so perfect. It should have had a dream ending."

Greta Dart, Magic Johnson's fifth-grade teacher, after he announced that he was HIV positive in November 1991

L ost in the bright glare of prosperity that illuminated U.S. sports and society during the 1990s were a surprising number of dark moments, most of them tinged with more than a hint of the surreal. In November 1991, Magic Johnson (*inset*), the talented and charismatic Los Angeles Lakers basketball star, stunned the world with the sobering announcement that he was HIV positive. Although he returned to play on the 1992 U.S. Olympic Dream Team and for parts of the 1995–96 NBA season, Johnson's illness was a wake-up call to a world still coming to grips with the growing epidemic.

Darker moments followed. On April 30, 1993, at a tennis tournament in Germany, Monica Seles, 19, was stabbed in the back by a deranged fan of Steffi Graf. The attacker, a German, later claimed that he stabbed Seles so she wouldn't supplant Graf as the world's number one player.

Then, following a 1994 practice session at the U.S. figure skating championships in Detroit, a man struck skater Nancy Kerrigan on the knee with a club. The assailant, a bodyguard of Kerrigan's rival Tonya Harding, and three other men, including Harding's husband, served prison sentences for their roles in the attack. Harding claimed no prior knowledge of the incident but was placed on probation and fined. Later, after it was revealed she knew more about the plot than she had admitted, she was banned for life from Olympic, world, and national competition.

Perhaps the oddest assault took place when former heavyweight champion Mike Tyson bit off part of Evander Holyfield's right ear in Round 3 of their June 1997 WBA bout. Tyson was disqualified seconds later when he bit Holyfield's left ear lobe.

The decade was also marked by untimely deaths. Tennis great Arthur Ashe died at 50 in 1993. New York Yankee legend Mickey Mantle died of liver cancer in 1995 at age 63. In 1998, former Olympic champion Florence Griffith-Joyner, only 38 and still the world record holder in the 100- and the 200-meter dashes, died of a seizure. In October 1999, golfer Payne Stewart, 42, a two-time U.S. Open champion, perished in an airplane accident in the heartland. Less than a week later, 45-year-old Walter Payton, the NFL's all-time leading rusher, succumbed to liver disease.

Intense rivalry between Tonya Harding (foreground) and Nancy Kerrigan (background) led to a plot intended to sabotage Kerrigan's career at the 1994 U.S. figure skating championships, where the two were competing for spots on that year's Olympic team.

Entrances and Exits

U pon his professional debut in 1996, the young Tiger Woods dominated the PGA Tour almost immediately, and he went on to earn the respect and awe of the entire sports world. It was perhaps fitting that one of his frequent playing partners when he wasn't competing was Michael Jordan, the only other athlete who had achieved similar stature—but who retired before Woods could steal his thunder. Seven months after dominating the final moments of Game Six of the 1998 NBA Finals against the Utah Jazz, Jordan, one of sports's all-time most dazzling performers, ended the greatest career in NBA history.

Though hockey star Wayne Gretzky, with 61 National Hockey League scoring records, didn't end his mind-boggling 21-year career with a victory, he still went out a hero. After the Rangers lost to the Pittsburgh Penguins 2–1, Gretzky, having played his last game, acknowledged a standing ovation from the New York crowd by skating around the rink with tears in his eyes.

As several football legends played their last seasons—Joe Montana ('94), John Elway ('98), Barry Sanders ('98), Dan Marino ('99), Steve Young ('99)—a new generation of stars emerged. Green Bay's Brett Favre won three MVP trophies, and young-gun Peyton Manning of Indianapolis spurred a football renaissance for the Colts. In baseball, a new breed of power-hitting shortstop, led by Seattle's Alex Rodriguez and New York's Derek Jeter, filled the superstar void left by Hall of Famers George Brett and Nolan Ryan, who both took their leave in '93.

Although women's tennis bid farewell to nine-time Wimbledon champion Martina Navratilova ('94) and Grand Slam-winner Steffi Graf ('99), the sport gained new popularity with the maturing of powerful young players such as Venus and Serena Williams.

After three unsuccessful trips to the Super Bowl, John Elway (above) and the Broncos prevailed over the Green Bay Packers, 31–24, in 1998. Said announcer Pat Summerall: "John Elway is the master of the inconceivable pass thrown to the unreachable spot."

Martina Navratilova (inset) celebrates a record ninth Wimbledon championship in 1990. Her superb conditioning, as well as her aggressive serve-and-volley game, set the tone for a generation of players that followed. She ended her 22-year career in 1994.

At the 1998 Australian Open, Serena Williams (left), 16, and Venus Williams, 17, compete as doubles partners. Even before either one won a singles title, the sisters commanded the attention of competitors and fans. In 1997 Venus was the first unseeded player of the modern era to make it to the finals of the U.S. Open, and in '99, Serena won the U.S. Open, defeating top-seeded Martina Hingis. (Venus won her first Grand Slam in 2000, at Wimbledon.)

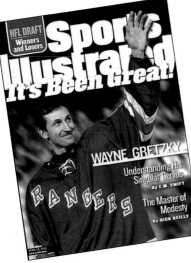

The April 26, 1999, Sports Illustrated cover (left) trumpets the retirement of the Great One, hockey legend Wayne Gretzky. Gretzky's career produced an unprecedented array of NHL records: At decade's end, he was the all-time leader in goals, assists, and total points, and had 10 of the 15 most prolific seasons in NHL history.

Game of Hard Knocks

Pro football's most successful team in the 1980s—the San Francisco 49ers, with four Super Bowl victories—went on to become the first team ever to win five Super Bowls. But in the years before quarterback Steve Young led the 49ers to that record-setting victory in 1995 (*inset*), fans watched the talented Buffalo Bills play in four straight Super Bowls—and lose each time. It was a riveting, if heartbreaking, show of excellence.

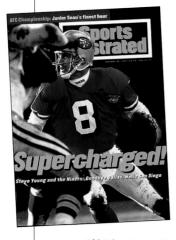

A tense 20–19 loss to the New York Giants in 1991's Super Bowl—a game the Bills would have won if kicker Scott Norwood had made a last-second, 47-yard field-goal attempt— left the Bills confident they had what it takes to make it back to the big game. They were right: The next season they faced Mark Rypien and the Washington Redskins but emerged as Super Bowl losers yet again.

In '93, AFC champs again, the Bills were routed 52–17 by the explosive Dallas Cowboys, led by quarterback Troy Aikman, wide receiver Michael Irvin, and running back Emmitt Smith. Undaunted, the Bills returned in '94, only to lose to the Cowboys again, 30–13. Buffalo's quarterback, Jim

"We're not a city of losers anymore . . . it's been a long, hard road for all of us."

Tyrone Braxton, of the Denver Broncos, after winning Super Bowl XXXII

Kelly, spoke for the entire AFC, which had not won a Super Bowl in 14 years, when he said, "What did I do to deserve this?"

In 1998 the NFC's winning streak finally ended when the Denver Broncos defeated the Green Bay Packers 31–24. The victory was especially sweet for Broncos quarterback John Elway, who had played in three Super Bowls in the 1980s but had yet to win. The Broncos successfully defended their title the following year, giving Elway the career capper he deserved.

Of course, it's worth noting that the Hall of Fame is littered with brilliant players who never won a Super Bowl. The '90s saw two surefire inductees depart the game similarly titleless: Barry Sanders of Detroit and Dan Marino of Miami.

Emmitt Smith of the Dallas Cowboys runs against Pittsburgh in Super Bowl XXX (above). The 1996 game, which Dallas won 27–17, drew an estimated 750 million television viewers.

One of football's rising stars in the '90s, Green Bay quarterback Brett Favre (right) led the Pack to consecutive Super Bowls in '97 and '98.

"The Games will go on. I repeat, the Games will go on . . . the Games will go on."

François Carrard, deputy general of the International Olympic Committee, after the bombing in Atlanta's Centennial Park

Tara Lipinski shows perfect form during the free skate program that won her a gold medal at Nagano's Winter Olympics in 1998. At 15, she was the youngest person ever to win an Olympic figure-skating title.

The Olympics Turn Pro

In the 1990s the Olympic establishment finally abandoned its outdated standards of amateurism, allowing professionals to compete in the games. No athletes took greater advantage of this decision than U.S. basketball players. At the 1992 Barcelona Games, the United States fielded a basketball Dream Team of NBA legends. The team

On day 14 of the 1996 Olympic Games in Atlanta, Michael Johnson (left) wins the 200-meter dash, then looks over in amazement at the board announcing his world-record time.

Members of the 1992 Dream Team (below, from left), Charles Barkley, Magic Johnson, Patrick Ewing, Michael Jordan, and Karl Malone, helped the U.S. win the gold in basketball. The world had never seen such a collection of basketball talent in the same uniform.

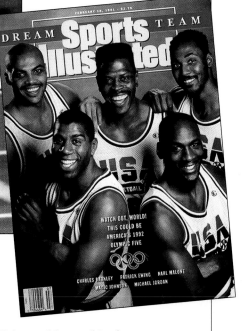

was so good it seemed unfair: The U.S. players awed fans and opponents with their spectacular athleticism and teamwork, winning their games by an average of 43 points and defeating Croatia 117–85 for the gold medal.

The 1996 games were briefly and horribly interrupted by a terrorist bombing at Atlanta's Centennial Park, in which two people died and 111 were injured. But the athletes who persevered left happier memories. Gymnast Kerri Strug landed a near-perfect vault on an injured ankle to help the U.S. clinch its first-ever team gold medal. Sprinter Michael Johnson became the first man in history to win the gold in the 200- and 400-meter dashes, shaving 0.34 second off the world record in the 200.

Stirring stories abounded at the '94 Winter Games as well, though none were as heartwarming as the saga of world champion speed skater Dan Jansen. Hours after his sister died of leukemia in 1988, Jansen tumbled to the ice at the Calgary Games. He came up empty again at Albertville, but in '94 at Lillehammer, he finally struck gold with a world-record time in the 1,000 meters.

Disastrous Proportions

★

EVENTS THAT TRANSFIXED THE WORLD

The rise of 24-hour news channels and the media's growing ability to be on the scene of an event at what seemed like a moment's notice created a hunger for spectacle in the '90s. It began with the televised Senate confirmation hearings of Supreme Court nominee Clarence Thomas in the fall of 1991. Because TV was there for the R-rated allegations—that Thomas had sexually harassed a former assistant, Anita Hill—America tuned in, even from the workplace.

So relentless was the media in its search for pithy sound bites and shocking images that by decade's end the media itself had come under scrutiny, accused of overstepping its rights and privileges. This was especially true when John F. Kennedy Jr. and his wife and sister-in-law were killed in a plane crash off Martha's Vineyard in 1999. News organizations were tenacious in their coverage of the tragedy and the grieving Kennedy family. Or was the media merely giving the people what they wanted? For no matter how tragic or scandalous or shocking the news—and in the '90s such news was abundant—the public's response was the same: to remain glued to the TV set.

Clarence Thomas (left) answers questions about Anita Hill's charges of sexual misconduct. Flowers and mementos decorate a makeshift shrine (above) to John F. Kennedy Jr. outside his New York City apartment.

Helicopters buzz over the compound as part of the constant effort to harass the Davidians into surrendering.

On the sixth day of the siege at the Branch Davidian compound, agents of the U.S. Bureau of Alcohol, Tobacco and Firearms keep surveillance next to a bulldozer blocking an approach road.

"We are ready for war. Let's get it on. Your talk is becoming vain."

David Koresh, during the siege in Waco

Fiery End at Waco

Federal and state law-enforcement officials had been watching the Branch Davidian compound near Waco, Texas, for months before they raided it in February 1993. The Davidians, an obscure group of religious extremists that split from the Seventh-Day Adventists years before, were believed to be engaged in cult behavior and amassing illegal weapons. And the government, sensitive to the growing numbers of survivalist and paramilitary groups, was still feeling the effects of the standoff at Ruby Ridge, Idaho, one year earlier, when federal marshals exchanged fatal fire with a separatist family.

Leading the Davidians was 34-year-old high-school dropout David Koresh, who claimed to be the second Messiah. Koresh attracted over 100 followers, whom he prepared for an apocalyptic battle against unbelievers by stockpiling food and weapons and barricading the group in a compound that they ominously dubbed Ranch Apocalypse. On February 28, 1993, the Davidians used their arsenal to repel the raid by more than 100 agents of the U.S. Bureau of Alcohol, Tobacco and Firearms, killing four of them.

The FBI immediately began a 51-day siege intended to dislodge the Davidians. Koresh, who released 37 members at one point, repeatedly reneged on promises to surrender. Finally, at dawn on April 19, government tanks stormed the compound and tear gas was pumped in. The tumult ended hours later when Ranch Apocalypse suddenly caught fire. Koresh and 80 others, nearly one-third of them children, lost their lives in the blaze, which may have been started by the Davidians themselves, or the result of tanks knocking over lanterns or propane canisters.

For years, people questioned the outcome at Waco: Who started the fire? Were members, including children, shot by other Davidians before the blaze reached them? Was the government out of line from the beginning?

Black smoke and flames billow from the Branch Davidian compound in Waco, Texas. Millions watched on television as the blaze ended in more than 80 deaths.

Rubble from the World Trade Center's basement clutters the sidewalk in lower Manhattan; the bombing quickly became a symbol of Americans' diminished feelings of security at home following the 1993 attack by Muslim extremists.

Terror Hits Home

To a small group, America the beautiful became America the enemy during the '90s. At various times throughout the decade, individuals accused the country of being an infidel, a brute, and a technology monster. To strike a blow against their nemesis, they resorted to the worst acts of terrorism ever committed on U.S. soil.

On February 26, 1993, a Muslim extremist, part of a group waging "holy war" against perceived enemies of Islam, parked a van loaded with explosives in the underground garage of New York's World Trade Center and detonated it, killing six and injuring 1,000.

In Oklahoma City on April 19, 1995, a truck loaded with bombs and parked outside the nine-story Murrah Federal Building went off, demolishing the building and killing 169 and injuring 614. The explosion was the work of Gulf War veteran Timothy McVeigh, who wanted to make a statement against the government.

By mailing bombs that killed three people and wounded 23 over 18 years, Ted Kaczynski (the Unabomber) wanted to show that humankind was being destroyed by society's overemphasis on technology. The former math professor was captured after the *New York Times* agreed to publish his 35,000-word manifesto. David Kaczynski, of Schenectady, New York, read the diatribe, recognized the ideas in it as those of his older brother, Ted, and contacted the authorities.

Timothy McVeigh (above), the man behind the 1995 bombing in Oklahoma City that killed 169 people, including 19 children, ended up in the same federal maximum-security prison—Supermax—as Ted Kaczynski, who managed to elude authorities for 18 years. Kaczynski, dubbed the Unabomber by the FBI because his early targets were at universities, lived in Montana (his mailbox is below), far away from the civilization he so despised.

"Trial of the Century"

From the beginning—a surreal, low-speed, live-on-TV chase between one-time pro football star O. J. Simpson, in a white Bronco, and a phalanx of police cars on the Los Angeles freeway in June 1994—it was obvious that the country was in for a singular event. Simpson, America's favorite running back—a Heisman Trophy winner who managed to escape a life of crime and gangs to become a football legend and an actor and a sportscaster—was the prime suspect in a murder case. Simpson's former wife Nicole Brown Simpson and her friend Ronald Goldman had been stabbed to death outside her home in west Los Angeles.

The case went to trial with Simpson facing mountains of incriminating evidence and the cameras continuing to roll. The nation watched transfixed as testimony revealed that Simpson, so well liked and affable, had a history of spousal abuse and that detectives found the blood of both victims and the suspect on the driveway of Simpson's Brentwood estate and the dashboard of his Bronco. They never recovered the murder weapon, but they did find a bloodstained glove on Simpson's property. His "Dream Team" of lawyers, assembled by lawyer-to-the-stars Robert Shapiro and headed by Johnnie Cochran, a charismatic trial lawyer who had built a career on defending minority victims of police misconduct, suggested that the glove may have been planted and blood samples contaminated. When a key prosecution witness, Los Angeles police detective Mark Fuhrman, lied under oath about his long record of racist behavior, the key issue became not innocence or guilt but race—and it divided the nation. On October 3, 1995, the jury ruled Simpson not guilty. Blacks were jubilant, whites were stunned, and the media—the only winner while the epic trial lasted—was bereft.

Simpson later won custody of his and Nicole's two children from Nicole's parents, but in civil suits brought by the victims' families in 1995 and 1997, juries found Simpson responsible for the deaths. He was ordered to pay the families a total of $33.5 million.

Flanked by his lead lawyers, Johnnie Cochran (left) and Robert Shapiro (right), Simpson reacts to prosecution arguments concerning the admissibility of spousal-abuse evidence against him.

> ## "I am the most important witness in the trial of the century. If I go down, their case goes bye-bye."

Mark Fuhrman, detective, Los Angeles Police Department

Christopher Darden, deputy district attorney, wrote a book, In Contempt, after the trial.

Legendary trial lawyer F. Lee Bailey was part of Simpson's legal team.

Testimony by Los Angeles police detective Mark Fuhrman backfired on the prosecution.

Harvard law professor Alan Dershowitz served as Simpson's appellate specialist.

Lance Ito, presiding judge, was often accused of being "star-struck."

Marcia Clark, perceived as a steely prosecutor, had not lost a case in 10 years.

Kato Kaelin, aspiring actor and Simpson's boarder, testified about the night of the murders.

Robert Shapiro, lawyer to the stars, assembled Simpson's "Dream Team" of lawyers.

Johnnie Cochran, Simpson's lead attorney, was unflappable and could disarm witnesses.

Always graceful in the public eye, Diana, at a fund-raiser in Chicago, greets a throng of supporters in 1996.

Sons William (far left) and Harry (second from right) lead Diana's funeral procession with their father, Prince Charles (far right), and uncle Lord Charles Spencer. More than a million Brits lined the streets.

A sea of flowers stretches in front of the gates of Kensington Palace (opposite) in the week following Diana's death. Prime Minister Tony Blair called Diana "the people's princess."

The People's Princess

Perhaps no other '90s celebrity raised questions about the role and power of the media the way Princess Diana did. The media loved her because the people did. When she married Charles, Prince of Wales, in 1981, 750 million viewers watched on television, making the event among the most watched in history. But in 1997, after Diana was killed in a crash that involved her car being chased by overzealous paparazzi, people wondered if all the media attention had ultimately killed her.

Though the marriage to Charles didn't last, the public's

"I'm lucky . . . I have found my role . . . I love being with people."

Princess Diana

love affair with Diana did, and the media dutifully, perhaps obsessively, covered it. There was the birth and raising of her two sons, William and Harry; her failing marriage; campaigning for the removal of land mines in Bosnia; promoting AIDS research; running errands in London. When she took up with the wealthy Egyptian Dodi al-Fayed, whose father owned real estate around the world, the media was there for that too, ignoring Diana's pleas for privacy. In Paris on August 30, 1997, the pair dined at Fayed's father's Hotel Ritz and then raced off into the night, reporters in pursuit. Their car sped into a tunnel and crashed. The driver (later found to have been drunk and on antidepressants) and Fayed were killed instantly; bodyguard Trevor Rees-Jones survived but was severely injured. Diana, 36, died in the hospital the next morning. Her funeral, broadcast live on television, was the most watched event in history, drawing an estimated 2.5 billion viewers worldwide.

Classroom Atrocities

Shock, horror, outrage, sorrow. People struggled in vain to come to terms with the feelings unleashed by two teenagers who, armed with an array of guns and bombs, entered their Colorado high school and killed 12 schoolmates and a teacher and wounded 38 before turning their guns on themselves. Though shocking, the April 20, 1999, incident was not the first involving young people, weapons, and violence at school. In 1996, in Moses Lake, Washington, a ninth grader had shot and killed three people. In the following eight months, students in West Paducah, Kentucky; Pearl, Mississippi; Jonesboro, Arkansas; and Springfield, Oregon, turned guns on their classmates. The assailants, all boys 11 to 16 years old, killed 15 people and wounded 44. But the incident at Columbine High School in Littleton, Colorado—where students trapped inside cowered under desks and crowded into small spaces, saying their prayers and trying not to cry—would torment adults and frighten children for a long time. Why did Eric Harris, 18, and Dylan Klebold, 17, plan what they called their "Judgment Day"? How could they amass an arsenal of weapons and make five hate-filled videos without raising suspicions? Ultimately, blame for the outbursts fell variously on parents, violent video games (Harris and Klebold loved the intensely destructive Doom), the media, social pressures, and the easy accessibility of guns.

Students and police crouch behind a car outside Columbine High School (above). Opposite, from left, Rhianna Cheek, Mandi Annibel, and Rachel Roof comfort one another during a candlelight vigil in honor of the students and teacher killed at Columbine.

Variations on a Pop Theme

★

MUSIC'S MASS APPEAL

With new trends emerging almost yearly, pop music in the '90s was—depending on your point of view—dynamic and diverse or diffuse and fragmented. One critic dubbed the decade's music "the age of everything." Certainly people were listening: In 10 years the number of CDs shipped annually more than quadrupled to nearly one billion. New forms like grunge grabbed the spotlight, while older forms like hip-hop and country surged in popularity. Galvanized by the sexy gyrations of Puerto Rican-born Ricky Martin (*right*) and other new Spanish-speaking artists singing in English, Latin pop enjoyed a wider audience too. Teen pop, practiced most notably by the Backstreet Boys, appealed enormously to preadolescents. For a time, Hootie & the Blowfish—"nice clean-cut boys," as one suburban mom described the group—was ascendant, appealing to both baby boomers and their children.

The diverse pop pantheon was increasingly populated by divas. The all-women tour known as Lilith Fair graced the rock-festival circuit from 1997 to 1999. Alanis Morrisette's *Jagged Little Pill* led all single-album sales. And only Garth Brooks (*left*) sold more albums during the '90s than those superdivas of pop, Mariah Carey and Celine Dion.

Enthusiastic fans propelled Garth Brooks (left) into the all-time-greatest ranks. Though a country singer, he had a pop-music style and sported a clean-cut look.

Rock's Disgruntled Youth

Young fans groove to the music at Lollapalooza (top), a multigroup nationwide tour that featured grunge music from bands like Nirvana, Soundgarden, and Pearl Jam (inset).

Sub Pop Records, the independent-label Seattle record company that helped launch groups such as Nirvana, Soundgarden, and Alice in Chains, dubbed the groups' new sound "grunge." The name derived from the look as much as the music. The rebellious young rockers who played in the bars of Seattle at the beginning of the decade wore shabby flannel shirts and torn jeans. More than any other group, Nirvana, with its heavy-metal chords and punk iconoclasm, typified grunge. Singer-lyricist Kurt Cobain, who formed the band with a high-school friend in 1987, wore his hair long and bleached blond or dyed pink. He jerked around the stage as if being electrocuted, and attacked the sound system to generate ear-splitting feedback. On the single "Smells Like Teen Spirit," he howled the pain of a new generation.

Other bands, notably Pearl Jam, followed with their own litanies of youthful despair and helped boost the grunge subculture into the wider public eye. As a result of increased radio play, grunge groups inevitably found themselves part of the pop mainstream they had rejected. "Teenage angst has paid off well / Now I'm bored and old," sang Cobain on Nirvana's second hit album, *In Utero*. In 1994, alienated and addicted to heroin, he wrote, "It's not fun for me anymore," and then put a shotgun to his head. Like an earlier Seattle poet of pain, Jimi Hendrix, Cobain was only 27 when he died.

Nirvana, led by the angst-energized Kurt Cobain (center), who committed suicide in 1994, was the first band to put grunge on the charts. Chris Novoselic (top) and David Grohl (right) were also part of the trend-setting group, which got its start in Seattle.

The solo success of Lauryn Hill (above, with fellow Fugees Prakazrel Michel, left, and Wyclef Jean) proved there's more to hip-hop than rapping. Her 1998 album sold more than 400,000 copies its first week.

Busta Rhymes (left) anticipated the millennium with his third album, Extinction Level Event—The Final World Front, released in 1998. Known for his wordplay and outrageous style, Rhymes ventured into film acting and started his own clothing company.

Listeners Take the Rap

The popularity of rap and hip-hop music was as apparent on the streets as it was on the radio and in album sales. The rhythmic speech of rap, and rap that was set to music (hip-hop), moved urban and suburban youth across the country to adopt a look (low-slung pants, baseball cap turned backward, hair braided in dreadlocks) and express an attitude that resembled nothing that rock, country, or any other popular music had ever inspired. Both the sound and style of rap reached its apogee in wordplay master Busta Rhymes of Brooklyn.

A subculture of violence haunted the hip-hop world, however. Gangsta rap gloried in images of ghetto rage, sexism, and degradation, and some of its most prominent practitioners got entangled in criminal affairs. Gangsta rappers Dr. Dre and Snoop Dogg were implicated in violent crimes, though they were not convicted. Two others, Tupac Shakur and Notorious B.I.G. (Christopher Wallace), were killed in drive-by shootings.

Happier vibes emanated from hip-hop's Fugees, who came from New Jersey. The group chose its name, which is short for *refugees*, because two members of the trio—Wyclef Jean and Prakazrel Michel—had roots in Haiti. The Fugees' 1996 album, *The Score*, sold 18 million copies worldwide and proved that hip-hop, which was derived from reggae and soul, could outsell gangsta rap.

The Fugees' third member, Lauryn Hill, who joined the group in 1988 when she was only 13, struck out on her own 10 years later and achieved stunning success. She wrote, produced, and performed her first solo album, the ironically titled *The Miseducation of Lauryn Hill*. By blending soul, reggae, hip-hop, gospel, even a little doo-wop, the album showcased her singing as much as her rapping, and demonstrated that Ms. Hill had not been miseducated at all.

"Either you're going to be a part of it or you're going to be conquered by it. Hip-hop is a forever thing."

Busta Rhymes, in an interview with MTV

The rise of gangsta rap raised questions about the relationship between music and violence. One of two gangsta rappers killed in drive-by shootings, Tupac Shakur, at left with Snoop Dogg and in the mural above, was a formally trained actor who was nominated for an NAACP award. Snoop Dogg, a role model to ghetto youth, had numerous run-ins with the law.

Another Country

Country music sounded a lot like pop when Garth Brooks released *Ropin' the Wind* in 1991. The album became the first ever to debut atop both the country and pop charts, and Brooks became the top-selling pop artist of the decade, with 60 million albums sold. With clean-cut cowboy looks, Brooks sang songs that had little in common with the drinkin' and cheatin' tunes that had long been associated with country music.

The emergence of a new generation of female singers further blurred the distinction between country and pop. Double- and triple-platinum albums by Faith Hill (*right*)—whose cover-girl looks, and the cosmetics endorsements to go with them, brought high fashion to country—pushed the boundaries of pop. Canadian-born Shania Twain was known for her showmanship and sexy outfits. Twain, who raised her three younger siblings after their parents died in an auto crash, changed her name from Eilleen to Shania, which in the Ojibwa language of her stepfather means "I'm on my way." Her 1997 album *Come on Over* was the second-best-selling album of the decade by any artist, country or pop.

Only young LeAnn Rimes, just 13 when her album *Blue* crashed both the country and pop charts in 1996, managed to find pop success without totally abandoning her country roots. Fans said she sounded like country legend Patsy Cline.

"You can't please everyone. As long as I'm comfortable and like what I see in the mirror, I go for it."

Shania Twain, songwriter and vocalist

While the newest female vocalists redefined country's image, one—young LeAnn Rimes (left)—kept the traditionalists happy. Shania Twain (right) emphasized feminism and femininity in her lyrics. The Grammy-winning songwriter, whose album The Woman in Me sold more than 10 million copies, honed her craft in Canada.

Garth Brooks (left) was on his way to becoming the biggest recording artist of all time. His 1991 album Ropin' the Wind was the first ever to debut atop both the country and pop charts.

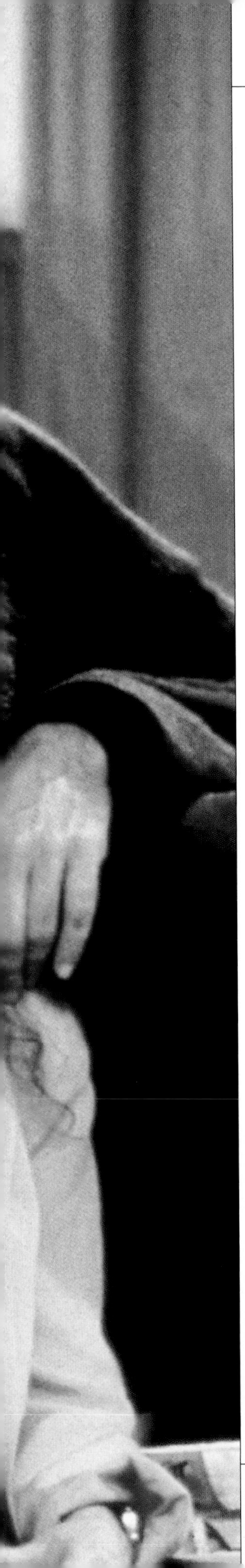

Programmed to Compete

★

BIG HITS ON THE SMALL SCREEN

Despite the increased competition from cable, which drew large teen and twenty-something audiences, traditional broadcast television proved it could still earn high marks. Veteran networks ABC, CBS, and NBC weren't the most creative, but they won large audiences with shows like *ER* and *NYPD Blue,* and they revived the daytime talk-show format. Proving that the medium had room for innovation were the upstart networks Fox and WB— with shows like *Ally McBeal* (starring Calista Flockhart, *below,* as a quirky lawyer) and the animated *Simpsons.* The cable channels flourished, especially HBO, whose *Sopranos,* about Mafia life, and *Sex in the City,* about just that and four single women in New York, brought in more than a million new subscribers. ABC, CBS, and NBC, meanwhile, went looking for comedians.

Of the several stand-up comics who were given shows, one emerged as a phenomenon: Jerry Seinfeld. With former stand-up comedian Larry David, he created *Seinfeld,* about four neurotic, self-absorbed friends (the comedian played a fictional version of himself) who lived in New York and contended with the more trivial aspects of daily life. After its debut on NBC in May 1990, *Seinfeld* became one of the most popular sitcoms of all time. From 1993 on, it never fell below the third spot in the Nielsen rankings, and a remarkable 76 million people

The cast of NBC's Seinfeld (left) featured (from left) Jason Alexander, Jerry Seinfeld, Michael Richards, and Julia Louis-Dreyfus.

watched the final episode when it aired in May 1998. Tim Allen's *Home Improvement* (ABC, 1991) took off from his stand-up routine by featuring Allen as a husband, father, and bumbling he-man host of a home-repair show. Over its eight seasons, the show was regularly ranked in the top 10. In 1996 CBS pulled Ray Romano off the stage and onto *Everybody Loves Raymond*. NBC also found a show for Paul Reiser. Called *Mad About You*, it debuted in 1992 and starred Reiser and Helen Hunt as newlyweds.

Bucking the stand-up trend was NBC's smash ensemble comedy *Friends* (1994), featuring six young relative unknowns tackling single life in New York. *Friends* anchored NBC's power-house Thursday-night lineup, which included *Seinfeld* as well as the critically acclaimed comedy *Frasier*. Starring Kelsey Grammer as a psychiatrist with a call-in radio show, *Frasier* was spun off that old '80s favorite, *Cheers*.

Friends starred (top, from left) Courtney Cox Arquette, Matthew Perry, Jennifer Aniston, David Schwimmer, Lisa Kudrow, and Matt LeBlanc. The group often hung out at the Central Perk Café. (inset). Mad About You, with Paul Reiser and Helen Hunt (bottom), did not become a hit until its third season.

"We want the show to be about the problems no one is trained to handle."

Jerry Seinfeld, on his long-running sitcom, *Seinfeld*

Continuing a role he originated on Cheers, Kelsey Grammer (center) took psychiatrist Frasier Crane from Boston to Seattle, the setting for Frasier. The new show also featured (from left) Peri Gilpin, John Mahoney, David Hyde Pierce, and Jane Leeves.

The stars of Fox network's Beverly Hills 90210 graduate from West Beverly High School in 1993 (above, from left): Jason Priestley, Brian Austin Green, Tori Spelling, Shannen Doherty, and Ian Ziering.

New England was the setting for the influential coming-of-age series Dawson's Creek. Its stars were (from left) Joshua Jackson, Katie Holmes, James Van Der Beek, and Michelle Williams.

In the risqué Melrose Place, the characters played by Jack Wagner and Heather Locklear (right) carried on a volatile affair. The critics praised Party of Five, which starred (opposite, from left) Neve Campbell, Matthew Fox, twins Taylor and Brandon Porter (as the infant sibling), Scott Wolf, and Lacey Chabert.

Prime Time for Teens

The children of baby boomers, many of whom were entering their teens in the '90s, were a huge market for broadcast television programmers at a time when cable, with more and more channels and viewers, was putting the squeeze on network TV. Teen

"Before 90210, 90 percent of American [teens on TV] were pets . . . little comic relief adjuncts."

Robert Thompson, director, Center for the Study of Popular Television, Syracuse University

shows ranged from the somber, critically acclaimed *My So-Called Life*, to the more formulaic but widely popular *Dawson's Creek*. The genre proliferated and had such revenue potential that the new prime-time networks Fox

and WB relied on teen shows to establish themselves.

Setting the trend in 1990 was Fox's *Beverly Hills 90210*, which chronicled the life and times of twins Brenda and Brandon Walsh at the most glamorous high school in the land. The show's success—it became the second-longest-running drama series of the decade—encouraged Fox to create a spin-off for twenty-some-things: the racy *Melrose Place*. Fox received critical acclaim for the less watched *Party of Five*, a Golden Globe–winning drama about five orphaned siblings trying to make it on their own.

The WB network, which began offering prime-time programming in 1995, mined the teen market with the horror-drama *Buffy the Vampire Slayer* (she had a love life); *Felicity*, about a young woman starting college; and *Dawson's Creek*, about four high-school friends. *Dawson's Creek* was so popular—eventually commanding $250,000 per commercial—in the fall of 1999 network programming included 10 shows with similar coming of age themes. But it wasn't all superficial. Many of these new dramas were the first to treat issues like teen pregnancy and substance abuse with seriousness and depth.

"On [TV] real life belongs to cops. Want to be a character with an adult life? Get a badge."

Lewis Cole, *The Nation*, October 25, 1993

The law-enforcement officers of the Broward County (Florida) Sheriff's Department were the focus of Cops (above) when it debuted in 1989. Other police departments around the country were later featured. The cast of NYPD Blue included (above right, from left) Jimmy Smits, Dennis Franz, and James McDaniel.

Shows Get Real

The successful crime series *Cops*, which followed real police officers and debuted on the Fox network in 1989, influenced all the networks. By mid-decade, several copycat series (such as *American Detective*, *True Detectives*, and *Secret Service*) had been launched, and television staples—shows about cops, docs, and lawyers—became more gritty and riveted viewers.

NBC's *ER*, conceived by best-selling novelist, screenwriter, and former Harvard medical student Michael Crichton *(Jurassic Park)*, depicted the stark realities of life in a Chicago hospital emergency room. The show debuted in 1994 and was the top-rated drama during each of its first six seasons. Woven into *ER*'s near-textbook-quality medical content, with its numerous heart-pounding crises, were subplots involving the personal lives of its characters. *Chicago Hope* (CBS, 1994) explored the complexities of hospital administration and bioethics with episodes that featured sticky moral and political issues like managed care and euthanasia.

Each episode of NBC's *Law & Order*, which first aired in 1990, told the story of a criminal investigation from arrest (the first half-hour) through prosecution (the second half). By its 10th season, 14 million viewers per week were drawn to its documentary style and realism. The violence and despair depicted in ABC's *NYPD Blue* (1993) were too much for many viewers, but the show attracted a large and loyal audience as well as critical praise, winning multiple Emmys during its first seven seasons.

The ensemble cast of the high-ranking ER included (from left) George Clooney, Eriq La Salle, Sherry Stringfield, and Anthony Edwards.

Figures of Speech

Jerry Springer *(left)* on *The Tonight Show with Jay Leno*, 1998

Republican presidential hopeful Elizabeth Dole *(right)* on *Larry King Live*

An era in late-night television came to an end when Johnny Carson handed the reigns of *The Tonight Show* to Jay Leno in 1992 after hosting TV's most profitable variety hour for 30 years. NBC's choice of hosts disappointed David Letterman, whose own popular talk show, *Late Night*, had followed Carson's for almost 10 years, a time slot held as the training ground for Johnny's heir apparent. CBS eventually hired Letterman, in '93, and for the first time in 39 years the long-running *Tonight Show* was seriously challenged: Younger viewers preferred Letterman to Leno.

This competition did not deter the entry of new talk shows or the reinvention of tried and true. Between 1986 and the 1996–97 season, the field grew from just a handful to 19. The most watched—and critically praised—of the new ones was daytime's *Rosie O'Donnell Show*, which debuted in 1996. Based on the old *Mike Douglas Show*, it won O'Donnell four consecutive Emmys for outstanding daytime talk-show host. In 1998 Oprah Winfrey added to her hugely popular program a segment called "Remembering Your Spirit"; designed to help viewers lead a more spiritual life, it offered inspirational words and practical suggestions. Larry King's long-running live show on CNN continued to feature newsy topics, while Charlie Rose's uninterrupted, hourlong interviews on PBS shook up the academic set with garrulous interviews with the likes of '60s notable Hunter S. Thompson and singer Aaron Neville.

Wearing the $3.5 million necklace made famous in 1997's Titanic, Kathie Lee Gifford (left) and Regis Philbin, of the decade-spanning a.m. talk show Live with Regis & Kathie Lee, re-create a scene from the movie. It was the first public wearing of the necklace, which was later auctioned to benefit AIDS research.

Host Rosie O'Donnell stands in front of an audience of 180 look-alikes. Nearly 2,000 people sent in photographs in an attempt to win a seat to the November 1996 show.

The Simpsons

Tooning In

The riskiest move in '90s prime-time television—the January 1990 debut of the animated show *The Simpsons* (*above*), on the Fox network—was actually not the first time a cartoon series was created for prime time. The first was in 1960, when *The Flintstones* began its six-year run. Both shows were about a family—the Simpsons had three children instead of one—and both had characters with square-shaped heads. But the similarities ended there.

The brainchild of Matt Groening, author of the twisted *"Life in Hell"* comic strip, the Simpsons first appeared in brief filler pieces on *The Tracey Ullman Show* in the late 1980s. With Homer J. Simpson, the bumbling patriarch; his wife, Marge; and their three children—Bart (*inset*), Lisa, and Maggie—the hilariously dysfunctional family struck a chord with adults and children alike. *The Simpsons* quickly became the fledgling Fox network's top show, and almost overnight other animated series began appearing all over TV's evening schedule.

The cable channels ventured into territory no regular network would go. Nickelodeon's *The Ren and Stimpy Show*, about a cat-and-mouse duo and originally intended for children, featured scatological humor that appealed to young adults. In 1993 MTV tested conventional limits with *Beavis and Butt-Head*, about two

Beavis and Butt-Head

South Park

King of the Hill

teenage ne'er-do-wells (*top*) who set fire to things, tortured animals, and rated music videos with a simple "this sucks" or "this is cool." The show eventually was moved from 7 p.m. to a more adult late-night slot.

Other prime-time animated series included *King of the Hill* (Fox), by *Beavis and Butt-Head* creator Mike Judge; *Dilbert* (UPN), about office life in the cubicle ranks; and *The Family Guy* (Fox), featuring another dysfunctional family—this one with a talking dog and baby. And just when it seemed that animators had gone as far as they could in their choice of subject matter, Comedy Central, another cable channel, released Matt Stone and Trey Parker's *South Park* (1997), about four third graders. What *South Park* lacked in animation style it more than made up for with episode topics like cloning, religion, and sexuality and with dialogue that was often risqué.

"[Beavis and Butt-Head are figures] in the tradition of such human sitcom characters as Ralph Kramden and Al Bundy."

Alex McNeil, author of *Total Television*

Matt Groening, creator of The Simpsons (opposite) named his characters—all but Bart—after his own family: parents Homer and Marge, and siblings Maggie and Lisa. Viewers—and Hollywood—so loved the potty-mouthed kids featured in South Park that the series led to a movie. The voices for both Beavis and Butt-Head were supplied by their creator, Mike Judge. Hank, the father of King of the Hill's Texas family sold propane and propane accessories.

Allergy medicine Allegra, by Aventis Pharmaceuticals

Michael Jordan for McDonald's

Adstravaganza

Television commercials, as always, reflected several cultural trends in the '90s. Taking their cue from the success of comedy shows like *Friends* and *Seinfeld*, many ad makers aimed their pitches at younger, single people and adopted humor or the rapid-fire, quick-cutting editing style made popular by music videos. Many

---

"Even if this year's [Super Bowl] game is a dud, count on the ads generating some excitement."

Dottie Enrico, *USA Today*, January 27, 1995

---

advertisers used animals—both real and computer-animated—to promote their products: A talking Chihuahua piped up, "Yo quiero (I want) Taco Bell"; polar bears on ice swilled Cokes; and croaking amphibians and reptiles hawked Budweiser beer for half the decade.

Madison Avenue's favorite human celebrity was

Coca-Cola's computer-animated polar bear

Taco Bell's talking Chihuahua

Michael Jordan. With a little help from Nike, Gatorade, Hanes, Quaker Oats, MCI, and McDonald's—all of whom signed the former Chicago Bulls star—Jordan was close to becoming the most recognizable person on the planet. Other memorable commercials featured a brewing love affair between two connoisseurs of Taster's Choice; dancers whose swing talents touted khakis by Gap; and a scene-stealing sock puppet hamming it up for Pets.com.

Pharmaceutical companies launched sweeping ad campaigns when federal restrictions on the television advertising of prescription drugs eased in 1997, turning allergy medicines like Claritin and Allegra into household names. By decade's end, only companies with an enormous advertising budget or an extremely optimistic CEO could afford airtime during the broadcast of an event like the Super Bowl, during which a 30-second commercial spot that cost $800,000 in 1990 increased to $2 million in 1999. Proving once again that a picture is worth a thousand words, the most successful Super Bowl commercials depended on visual puns.

Budweiser launched one of the most successful ad campaigns of the '90s during the 1995 Super Bowl. The popularity of the campaign's characters—croaking frogs (left)—led Budweiser to create commercials featuring chameleons who were jealous of the frogs' success.

Artistic Differences

★

ENTERTAINMENT DIVERSIFIES

Government funding for the arts dried up when the Republican Congress voted in 1995 to phase out the National Endowment for the Arts over a two-year period. Although the NEA ultimately survived, it was greatly diminished. As the artistic community sought new patrons, many entertainers also looked "outside the box," for inspiration and compensation, coming up with new ways of doing business and elevating, in some cases, what was previously considered alternative—or underground—into the mainstream.

Low-budget, independently produced films—or "indies"—enjoyed a newfound popularity; the most successful was *The Blair Witch Project* (*inset*), which was largely improvised over an eight-day shoot and presented deadpan as a chilling documentary. Although its budget was just $100,000, *Blair Witch* grossed an incredible $210 million worldwide in 1999. On the other extreme, innovations in digital technology broadened the palette of big-budget movies. Additionally, many directors adapted classic novels, chronicled historic events, and featured younger, more serious actors than ever before. Broadway audiences flocked to musical comedy revivals and also embraced new plays that tackled tough subjects. And the book world learned the power of TV, as a talk-show host selected instant bestsellers and helped reintroduce reading to the masses.

The Sundance Film Festival, founded by Robert Redford (left) and staged every January in the Utah mountain town of Park City, became a mecca for independent and low-budget '90s filmmakers.

Digital Mise en Scène

Special effects sold better than sex at cinema box offices; the decade's most popular movies depended on spectacular sleight of hand sparked by the revolution in digital technology. Filmmakers had only to imagine something—a gargantuan earthbound asteroid *(Armageddon)*, enormous alien space ships emitting apocalyptic rays *(Independence Day)*, flying cows *(Twister)*, a villain made of morphing molten metal *(Terminator 2: Judgment Day)*, even a cameo appearance by President John F. Kennedy *(Forrest Gump)*—and computers made it real.

Two of the biggest blockbusters, *Jurassic Park* and *Star Wars: Episode 1— The Phantom Menace,* relied on the technical wizardry of Industrial Light & Magic (ILM). Founded by George Lucas to help create the first *Star Wars* film, ILM burgeoned into the world's largest digital-production facility. Director Steven Spielberg used ILM for the computerized dinosaurs that populated his fictional Jurassic theme park. In Lucas's *Phantom Menace*, ILM was responsible for an astonishing 90 percent of the film's images, including the first all-digital principal character, Jar Jar Binks.

The most ambitious movie of the '90s from the production standpoint—James Cameron's *Titanic*—combined computer technology, awesome set construction, and an old-fashioned love story. For filming in

Jurassic Park

They Don't Make 'Em Like They Used To

In the era B.C. (before computers), every animated movie image had to be painstakingly drawn and painted by hand. Computers transformed the pencil sketches on a storyboard into finished film with such efficiency and finesse that even Disney went digital. Starting in 1995, with the megahit Toy Story, digital technology took over. The decade's other computer-animated hits were Toy Story 2, A Bug's Life, and Antz.

Terminator 2: Judgment Day

Titanic

A brave new world of digital special effects dissolved the barrier between filmmakers' imaginations and the screen, bringing extinct dinosaurs (above) back to life, visions of the future to fantastic, reality-bending heights (top right), and vintage ocean liners to scale (bottom right).

"I'm king of the world!"

James Cameron, at the end of his Oscar acceptance speech for best director for *Titanic* at the 70th annual Academy Awards in 1998

Baja, Mexico, Cameron built models of the 882-foot doomed ocean liner at nearly full scale. The illusion of sailing was supplied by the addition of digital water, and the spectacular sinking scenes were achieved with the help of stunt men and computerized special effects. True to its name, *Titanic* cost more than any film in history—$200 million—and also grossed more: At the end of the decade, worldwide receipts totaled nearly $2 billion. It won 11 Academy Awards in 1998, tying a record set by *Ben-Hur* in 1959 for the most Oscars ever awarded to a single film.

Romancing the Past

Many '90s filmmakers turned back the clock to find the stories they wanted to tell. Novels by Charlotte Brontë, Edith Wharton, and E. M. Forster as well as three by Henry James were all adapted to film. And the bard enjoyed a renaissance, as his life (*inset, Joseph Fiennes in Shakespeare in Love*) and several of his classic plays

inspired high-profile films with A-list actors.

The quest for cinematic gold also focused on refined, contemporary literature. Michael Ondaatje's novel *The English Patient*, was transformed by director Anthony Minghella into a stunning film that won the 1996 Academy Award for best picture.

Real life—or at least Hollywood's interpretation of it—inspired several provocative, historically based films, too. Steven Spielberg plumbed the events of World War II for two of his most memorable films, *Schindler's List*, based on a true Holocaust story, and the fictional *Saving Private Ryan.* Mel Gibson dramatized medieval Scottish hero William Wallace in his second directing effort, *Braveheart.* Spike Lee's *Malcolm X* chronicled the life of the black activist and civil-rights leader.

"Thirteenth-century battles could not have been a picnic."

Director Mel Gibson, on the combat scenes in *Braveheart*

Epic sagas from both fact and fiction graced the big screen, bringing '90s movie audiences adaptations of all but one of Jane Austen's six novels (Emma, left, was one), wars for independence, (above), tales of political figures (near right), and sagas of tragic love (far right).

Gwyneth Paltrow in *Emma*

Mel Gibson in *Braveheart*

Denzel Washington
in Spike Lee's *Malcolm X*

Ralph Fiennes and Kristin Scott Thomas
in *The English Patient*

Hollywood's New Elite

Every decade boasts its galaxy of new Tinseltown luminaries, but the new stars of the 1990s seemed to grow younger and glow brighter. Strong acting technique as well as beauty were attributes of successful young '90s actors, who were just as comfortable in sentimental, traditional teen flicks (Claire Danes in *William Shakespeare's Romeo and Juliet*, Gwyneth Paltrow in *Moonlight and Valentino*, Kate Winslet in *Titanic*), as they were in more quirky, substantial, and challenging fare (Cate Blanchett in the title role of *Elizabeth*, Ewan McGregor in the hard-boiled *Trainspotting*, and Minnie Driver in the mouth-watering *Big Night*.

High-school pals Ben Affleck and Matt Damon were catapulted to fame after the success of their haunting 1997 film, *Good Will Hunting*. Its screenplay—adapted from one of Damon's Harvard writing assignments—was also penned by the young actors, who were rewarded with both Golden Globe and Academy Awards for best screenplay. Affleck and Damon would go on to star in a whirlwind nine films before decade's end.

In this firmament, however, few of these new stars were more magnetic than Leonardo DiCaprio. Legend has it that DiCaprio's first name came about when his mother felt the first kick of pregnancy while looking at a da Vinci painting. His cinematic breakout role came in 1993 at

---

"You see how picky I am about my shoes, and they only go on my feet!"

Alicia Silverstone, as Cher, on the subject of her virginity in *Clueless*

Alicia Silverstone (above) launched the '90s catch phrase, "As if!" when she starred in the 1995 cult hit Clueless.

age 19 when he beat out 400 other hopeful actors for the chance to star in the adaptation of Tobias Wolff's *This Boy's Life*. Later that same year his phenomenal performance as Johnny Depp's mentally retarded little brother in *What's Eating Gilbert Grape?* earned him an Oscar nomination for best supporting actor. As the tragic young Jack Dawson in *Titanic*, he cemented his status as the big screen's leading male heartthrob.

Matt Damon (above, right) and Ben Affleck wrote and starred in Good Will Hunting. Claire Danes and Leonardo DiCaprio (top) appeared as the tragic teen lovers Romeo and Juliet.

Crazy Like a Fox

Jim Carrey, a one-time janitor and high-school dropout, became one of the highest-paid Hollywood stars of the 1990s. The kinetic comedian first scored in 1994 with Ace Ventura: Pet Detective for which he was paid $350,000; two years later, he commanded $20 million for The Cable Guy. In 1998 he earned critical ac-claim in The Truman Show as a man whose life, unbeknown to him, is the subject of a television show.

Popcorn, Please

Moviegoers in the '90s were treated to a wide range of subjects and themes— everything from the adventures of Austin Powers, an international spy who needed dental work to serial murder and psychological sparring in The Silence of the Lambs. New directors scored with quirky hits. Quentin Tarantino's drug-culture melodrama, Pulp Fiction, launched the comeback of John Travolta, while brothers Ethan and Joel Coen scored with Fargo, a bizarre and amusing tale of murder on the prairie. Box-office sales rose by 25 percent— one major reason was the prolific Tom Hanks, who starred in 10 films and won two best-actor Oscars in a row: one for an AIDS victim fighting discrimination in Philadelphia and the second for the simple but decent title character in Forrest Gump.

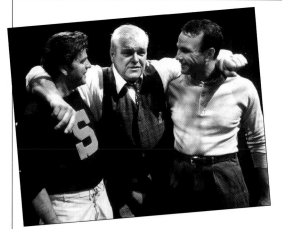

Brian Dennehy (above, center) appeared as Willy Loman in Arthur Miller's masterpiece, Death of a Salesman. It returned to the Great White Way 50 years after its Broadway debut. In adapting the animated film The Lion King (opposite) to the stage, theatrical visionary Julie Taymor made the production a visual symphony with her ingenious costume design and direction; she became the first woman to win the Tony award for best direction of a musical. Chita Rivera (below, center) returned to Broadway seven years after fracturing her leg in 12 places.

The Play's the Thing

Pulitzer Prizes for drama were awarded to works as varied as August Wilson's *The Piano Lesson* (1992), fifth in his cycle of plays covering the black experience in America decade by decade; Tony Kushner's *Angels in America: Millennium Approaches* (1993), the first of a two-part, seven-hour epic about AIDS, religion, and gay liberation in the Reagan era; and *Wit* (1999), Atlanta kindergarten teacher Margaret Edson's debut about a dying literature professor's final revelations.

Broadway broke its own box-office records with hits old and new. Musical revivals included such classics as *Guys and Dolls, Show Boat,* and *Kiss Me, Kate.* Although Andrew Lloyd Webber's *Cats* became the longest-running Broadway show, the onslaught of '80s British import musicals gave way to new American shows. *Ragtime* leaped from the pages of E. L. Doctorow's distinguished novel. *Bring in 'Da Noise, Bring in 'Da Funk (inset),* starring the virtuosic Savion Glover, brought a brilliant rhythm-and-tap

> ## "When people say, 'Break a leg,' I say, 'No thank you, I've already done that.' "
>
> Chita Rivera , star of 1993's *Kiss of the Spider Woman*

celebration of black history. Staged versions of animated Disney movies *The Lion King* and *Beauty and the Beast* helped transform Times Square into a family-friendly destination.

The rock opera *Rent,* loosely based on Puccini's *La Bohème,* revealed the talents of a new composer—but tragically late. Having given voice to the hopes and fears of the dispossessed young in New York's East Village, 35-year-old Jonathan Larson died of an aortic aneurysm hours before his musical's first public performance, in early 1996.

A Crowning Achievement

In 1993, Toni Morrison, Princeton University professor and author of six novels, was awarded fiction's highest citation, the Nobel Prize for Literature. She was the first black American and only the eighth woman to win the prize since it was instituted in 1901 by the Swedish Academy. In

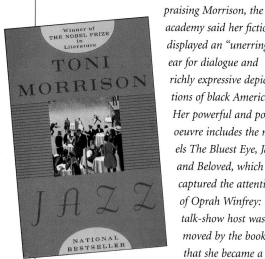

praising Morrison, the academy said her fiction displayed an "unerring ear for dialogue and richly expressive depictions of black America." Her powerful and poetic oeuvre includes the novels The Bluest Eye, Jazz, and Beloved, which captured the attention of Oprah Winfrey: The talk-show host was so moved by the book that she became a producer for the film version and starred in it, too. Winfrey also selected Song of Solomon and Paradise for her television book club, giving Morrison's work its widest audience yet. In addressing the importance of her identity as a black woman writer, Toni Morrison once said, "Had I lived the life that the state planned for me from the beginning, I would have lived and died in somebody else's kitchen, in someone else's land, and never written a word. That knowledge is bone deep, and it informs everything I do."

Page Turners

A new phenomenon rocked the fiction market in the 1990s—The Oprah Effect. The monthly segment of *The Oprah Winfrey Show* devoted to the star's TV "book club," first broadcast in 1996, helped catapult no fewer than 28 consecutive novels onto the bestseller list and made many of the authors very wealthy. Winfrey's stamp of approval carried so much weight that the very first book club selection, unknown author Jacquelyn Mitchard's *The Deep End of the Ocean*, exploded from an initial print run of 68,000 to an eventual four million.

Of course there were novelists who succeeded without Oprah's help. Attorney John Grisham turned the law-inspired novel into a commercial machine. Starting with *The Firm* in 1991, he would publish 10 wildly popular books before the decade's end; six would go on to be made into major motion pictures. And when she wrote *Harry Potter and the Sorcerer's Stone*, J. K. Rowling was a newly divorced single mother subsisting on welfare in an unheated Edinburgh flat. Harry, the enchanting 11-year-old wizard she created, performed extraordinary tricks of magic—not the least of which was to occupy the first, second, and third positions on the fiction bestseller list in Rowling's first three Harry Potter volumes.

On the literary front, American themes were prominent. John Updike completed his four-volume epic on middle-class living as experienced by the New England Everyman, Harry (Rabbit) Angstrom, while master novelist Philip Roth wrote what critics claimed was his finest work, the Pulitzer Prize-winning *American Pastoral*. Charles Frazier's debut effort—*Cold Mountain*, a gripping Civil War story—garnered many favorable reviews and had Hollywood knocking at his door.

Newcomer Frank McCourt, a retired New York City high-school English teacher, recalled growing up dirt poor in Ireland and his quest to make it to America in the poignant *Angela's Ashes*. It was the most notable example, perhaps, of the memoir, a genre made popular by an army of introspective '90s writers. *Into Thin Air*, Jon Krakauer's account of tragic disaster on Mount Everest, and *The Perfect Storm*, Sebastian Junger's harrowing story of a massive northeaster and a doomed fishing boat, both hit the nonfiction bestseller list and rekindled interest in adventure writing.

A diverse array of engrossing books (right) captivated the nation's hearts, minds, and pocketbooks during the 1990s.

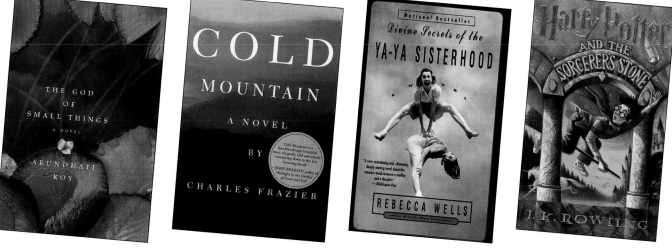

The Hundred Years' Bash

★

CELEBRATIONS WELCOMING THE 21ST CENTURY

A s the 1990s drew to a close, concern about the so-called "Y2K bug," a computer glitch caused by two-digit dating systems that treated the rollover to 2000 as if it were 1900 instead, grew to near hysterical proportions. Since nearly every aspect of humankind relied heavily on computers, predictions of major malfunctions—disappearing checking accounts, accidental missile launches, electrical blackouts, airline disasters—had some Americans preparing for apocalyptic chaos.

At the extreme were a few religious groups that, anticipating worldwide disruption, urged members to stockpile food. Some even perceived the end of the Cold War and the resulting spate of international conflicts as indicators of the impending apocalypse. Thankfully, the panic died down in the final two months of 1999, allowing the world to turn its attention to much happier matters—final preparations for a global bash to celebrate the arrival of the momentous year 2000.

The Republic of Kiribati in the South Pacific was the first to greet the new millennium, followed by New Zealand, and ending with French Polynesia. As millions of television viewers watched celebrations erupt around the globe—through all 24 time zones—the earth seemed suddenly a much smaller place.

A light show projects faces onto the ancient pyramids in Giza and serves as a backdrop to a New Year's concert (left). A Berlin retailer displays pairs of millennium glasses (inset) on sale for 25 German marks ($11).

The fireworks in Paris show off the City of Light with the Eiffel Tower as centerpiece. Paris spent three years preparing for its celebration, and at midnight, the tower became a giant sparkler (right) and appeared to take off like a rocket as fireworks erupted from its base for seven minutes.

London welcomes the year 2000 with the Continent's most magnificent and expensive fireworks celebration. Following the familiar midnight toll of Big Ben, 40,000 fireworks costing $1.5 million burst into the sky above the Thames River in the span of 15 minutes.

Times Square, always the site of major New Year's Eve celebrations, is a sea of balloons and confetti as New York City goes all out to mark the new millennium. This time, the ball that descended at midnight was made of crystal and the perennially large crowds swelled to three million.

A three-hour Hollywood extravaganza,
highlighted by a live performance by Will Smith
and an original film from Steven Spielberg,
preceded the millennium fireworks at the Washington Monument and the Reflecting Pool in
Washington, D.C.

ACKNOWLEDGMENTS

The editors wish to thank the following individuals and institutions for their valuable assistance in the preparation of this volume:

The staff of Bishop Books, New York, N.Y.: Morin Bishop, Barbara Chilenskas, Mary Arendt, Jia Baek, John Blackmar, Andrew Blais, John Bolster, Kate Brash, Ward Calhoun, Terry Deal, Lee Fjordbotten, Jeff Labrecque, Vincent Mejia, Jeanann Pannasch, Eve Peterson, and Ylann Schemm. Terrell Smith, Time-Life Books, Alexandria, Va.; Ronald Bailey, East Meredith, N.Y.; Charles Hagner, Alexandria, Va.; Time Inc. Picture Collection; Thomas Gilbert, TimePix; Norman Currie and Frederique Williams, Corbis; Jordan Tamagni, America Online.

PICTURE CREDITS

BIBLIOGRAPHY

BOOKS

Bellamy, Christopher. *Expert Witness: A Defense Correspondent's Gulf War 1990-91.* London: Brassey's, 1993.

Brewster, Todd, and Peter Jennings. *The Century.* New York: Doubleday, 1998.

Brunner, Borgna, ed. *1998 Information Please Almanac.* Boston: Houghton Mifflin, 1997.

Burns, James MacGregor, Georgia J. Sorenson, and Scott W. Webster. *Dead Center.* New York: Simon & Schuster, 1999.

Celebrate the Century: A Collection of Commemorative Stamps, 1990-1999. United States Postal Service, 2000.

Daniel, Clifton, ed. *Chronicle of the 20th Century.* Mount Kisco, N.Y.: Chronicle Publications, 1987.

Drew, Elizabeth. *On The Edge: The Clinton Presidency.* New York: Simon & Schuster, 1994.

Encyclopedia of World Biography. 2nd ed. Detroit: Gale, 1998.

Famighetti, Robert, ed. *The World Almanac and Book of Facts.* 1991-1999. Mahwah, N.J.: World Almanac Books, 1990-1998.

Freeze, Gregory L., ed. *Russia: A History.* New York: Oxford Univ. Press, 1997.

Glennon, Lorraine, ed. *Our Times: The Illustrated History of the 20th Century.* Kansas City, Mo.: Turner Publishing, 1995.

Gordon, Lois, and Alan Gordon. *The Columbia Chronicles of American Life 1910-1992.* New York: Columbia Univ. Press, 1995.

Gordon, Michael R., and General Bernard E. Trainor. *The Generals' War: The Inside Story of the Conflict in the Gulf.* Boston: Little, Brown, 1995.

Harvey, Edmund H., et al., eds. *Our Glorious Century,* Pleasantville, N.Y.: Reader's Digest, 1994.

Johnson, Otto, ed. *1997 Information Please Almanac.* Boston: Houghton Mifflin, 1996.

Kallen, Stuart A., (ed.). *A Cultural History of the United States Through the Decades: The 1990s.* San Diego: Lucent Books, 1999.

McNeil, Alex. *Total Television: The Comprehensive Guide to Programming from 1948 to the Present.* (4th ed.). New York: Penguin Books, 1996.

National Geographic Eyewitness to the 20th Century. Washington, D.C.: National Geographic, 1999.

Posner, Richard A. *An Affair of State: The Investigation, Impeachment, and Trial of President Clinton.* Cambridge: Harvard Univ. Press, 1999.

Stephanopoulos, George. *All Too Human: A Political Education.* Boston: Little, Brown, 1999.

Tomlinson, Joe. *The Ultimate Encyclopedia of Extreme Sports.* New York: Carlton Books, 1996.

Woodward, Bob. *Shadow: Five Presidents and the Legacy of Watergate 1974-1999.* New York: Simon & Schuster, 1999.

PERIODICALS

"After Newt." *Economist,* Nov. 14, 1998.

Alter, Jonathan. "Bright Newt, Fright Newt." *Newsweek,* Nov. 16, 1998.

Alter, Jonathan, et al. "Pressing the Flesh Online." *Newsweek,* Sept. 20, 1999.

Balz, Dan, and Molly Moore. "Bush Asks Nation to Back 'Defensive' Mission." *Washington Post,* Aug. 9, 1990.

Barrett, Jon. "The 1990s, Defining Moments of the Decade." *Advocate,* Jan. 18, 2000.

Beatty, Jack. "Fat and Mean." *Atlantic Monthly,* May 1996.

Bentrup, Nancy L., et al. "Thirty Years after Earth Day." *U.S. News & World Report,* Apr. 17, 2000.

Bowermaster, David, et al. "The Final Days of David Koresh." *U.S. News & World Report,* May 3, 1993.

Brackey, Harriet Johnson. "Hard-Charging GenXers Put Their Own Spin on Work." *San Diego Union-Tribune,* Mar. 27, 2000.

Branch, Shelly. "How Hip-Hop Fashion Won Over Mainstream America." *Black Enterprise,* June 1993.

Bronski, Michael. "After the 'Boom': Gay and Lesbian Book Publishing." *Publishers Weekly,* May 3, 1999.

Brown, Anitra. "Nike Spikes It." *Marketing and Media Decisions,* June 1990.

Brown, Eryn. "Valley of the Dollars." *Fortune,* Sept. 27, 1999.

Browne, Malcom W. "The Military vs. the Press." *New York Times,* Mar. 3, 1991.

Buechner, Maryanne, et al. "Digital 50: The Most Important People Shaping Technology Today." *Time Digital,* Oct. 4, 1999.

Bushnell, Davis. "'Body Art' Draws New Attention." *Boston Globe,* Apr. 30, 2000.

Carbonara, Peter, and Maggie Overfelt. "The Dot-Com Factories." *Fortune Small Business,* July-Aug. 2000.

Carter, Bill:
> "CNN Takes an Early lead in Coverage of the Gulf War." *New York Times,* Jan. 17, 1991.
> "Dawson's Clones." *New York Times,* Sept. 19, 1999.

Christian, Rebecca. "Gracious Living at Martha's Has Little to Do with Real Life." *Chicago Tribune,* May 2, 1993.

Cohen, Richard E. "The Rise and Fall of Newt." *National Journal,* Mar. 6, 1999.

Cohen, Richard E., and Marilyn Werber Serafini. "In the Eye of the House Hurricane." *National Journal,* Jan. 9, 1999.

Cooper, Matthew, and Howard Fineman. "Newt Hits the Showers." *Newsweek,* Nov. 16, 1998.

Croal, N'Gai, and Marty Katz. "Gadgets Galore, Large and Small." *Newsweek,* Jan. 18, 1999.

Davis, Sally Ogle. "Julia Roberts: Shooting Star." *Ladies Home Journal,* July 1991.

D'Innocenzio, Anne. "Cashing in on the Seventies Retro Rage." *Women's Wear Daily,* Nov. 20, 1997.

Dogar, Rana, et al. "Something Wireless This Way Comes." *Newsweek,* Oct. 11, 1999.

Elias, Justine. "Breaking Away: A Television Tradition." *New York Times,* Oct. 17, 1999.

Elliot, Stuart:
> "Super Bowl Is Attracting a Crowd of New Competitors." *New York Times,* Nov. 29, 1999.
> "Taco Bell Abruptly Drops the Agency." *New York Times,* July 19, 2000.

Entertainment Weekly, Nov. 1996-Apr. 2000.

Estes, Ashley. "Town Evacuated As Flood Pours Through Levee." *Associated Press,* Mar. 8, 1998.

Fischer, David, and Dan McGraw. "Designing for Dollars." *U.S. News & World Report,* Nov. 14, 1994.

Fong-Torres, Ben. "The New Faces of TV War." *San Francisco Chronicle,* Feb. 5, 1991.

Gallagher, John. "1999: The Year." *Advocate,* Jan. 18, 2000.

Gates, Anita. "Teenagers on TV." *New York Times,* Mar. 8, 2000.

Gest, Ted. "Congress and Cops." *U.S. News & World Report,* Dec. 26, 1994.

Golden, Daniel. "The New World: A Special Issue on Multiculturalism." *Boston Globe,* Oct. 13, 1991.

Goldman, John J. "Two Found Guilty in Bombing of Trade Center." *Los Angeles Times,* Nov. 13, 1997.

Grant, James. "*ER:* The Show That Gives Us Thursday Night Fever." *Cosmopolitan,* May 1995.

Gregory, Deborah. "Hip-Hop Fashion." *Essence,* Nov. 1992.

Griffin, Linda Gillan. "Victoria's Secret is Out." *Houston Chronicle,* Feb. 5, 1999.

Grover, Mary Beth. "Rules of the Game." *Forbes,* Dec. 27, 1999.

Halstead, Ted. "A Politics for Generation X." *Atlantic Monthly,* Aug. 1, 1999.

Hanson, Gayle M. B. "The Violent World of Video Games." *Insight on the News,* June 28, 1999.

Heilbrunn, Jacob. "Globalization's Boosters and Critics." *National Interest,* Fall 1999.

Hickey, Mary C., and Lynn Langway. "Supertrends." *Ladies Home Journal,* Nov. 1995.

Homer, Steve. "Switch On and Take Over the World." *Independent,* Dec. 21, 1992.

Huang, Thomas and Stephen Power. "Survival and Sorrow." *Dallas Morning News,* Apr. 22, 1995.

Hunt, Karyn. "Thousands March in San Francisco, New York Gay Pride Parades." *Associated Press,* July 1, 1996.

Ivanovich, David. "Plan Would Split Microsoft in Half." *Houston Chronicle,* Apr. 29, 2000.

Kalajian, Douglas. "Toy Crazy." *Palm Beach Post,* Dec. 9, 1998.

Kaplan, David A. "Anatomy of a Debacle." *Newsweek,* Oct. 21, 1991.

Kaplan, Lawrence F. "A Bridge Too Far." *National Interest,* Fall 1999.

Keegan, Paul. "Culture Quake." *Mother Jones,* Nov. 1, 1999.

Kerwin, Kathleen, and David Leonhardt. "Hey Kid, Buy This!" *Business Week,* June 30, 1997.

Kirp, David L. "Stranger Among Us." *Nation,* Sept. 9, 1996.

Klein, Joe. "The New, New Deal." *Newsweek*, Dec. 26, 1994.
Lagerfeld, Steven. "What Main Street Can Learn From the Mall." *Atlantic Monthly*, Nov. 1995.
Lawson, Carol. "Magic and Money." *New York Times*, Feb. 15, 1990.
Leibovich, Mark, Jeanne Dugan, and Tim Smart. "Internet's E-conomy Gets Real." *Washington Post*, June 20, 1999.
Levine, Joshua. "The Java News." *Forbes*, May 22, 1995.
Levy, Steven. "We're Running Out of Dot.Coms." *Newsweek*, Oct. 11, 1999.
Life, July 1993-June 1995.
"Lost in Cyberspace." *Economist*, Dec. 18, 1999.
McFadden, Robert. "Explosion at the Twin Towers." *New York Times*, Feb. 27, 1993.
McGonigle, Steve, and Gayle Reaves. "Ties To Terror." *Dallas Morning News*, June 8, 1997.
McLeod, J. O. "Making Fun: Martha Stewart Satirized in Magazine." *Times-Picayune*, Dec. 9, 1994.
Martin, Ed. "Programming Gets Real." *Inside Media*, Mar. 6, 1991.
Mashberg, Tom. "Welcome to 2000." *Boston Herald*, Jan. 1, 2000.
Masland, Tom. "Saddam Menaces Kuwait Again." *Newsweek*, Oct. 17, 1994.
Mason, Julie Cohen. "Workplace 2000." *Management Review*, Jan. 1993.
Mathews, Tom. "The Secret History of War." *Newsweek*, Mar. 18, 1991.
Max, D. T. "The Oprah Effect." *New York Times*, Dec. 26, 1999.
Melvin, Chuck. "Official Professor P.D.'s Unchallenged Greatest Computer Games of the Last Millennium." *Plain Dealer*, Mar. 6, 2000.
Mifflin, Lawrie. "They're New, They're Competitive." *New York Times*, Aug. 27, 1995.
Morganthau, Tom. "The Price of Neglect." *Newsweek*, May 11, 1992.
Mydens, Seth. "O.J. Simpson's Ex-Wife Slain At Her Condo in Los Angeles." *New York Times*, June 14, 1994.
Nemec, Richard. "What's New? Everything." *Communication World*, Aug. 1, 1999.
Newcomb, Peter, and Christopher Palmeri. "Throw a Tantrum, Sign a Contract." *Forbes*, Aug. 20, 1990.
Newman, Richard J. "Warfare 2020." *U.S. News & World Report*, Aug. 5, 1996.
Newquist, Harvey P., III. "Making AI Safe for Democracy." *AI Expert*, June, 1991.
Newsweek, Nov. 1993-2000.
Nielson, Jakob. "Pooped Peepers." *Forbes*, Dec. 4, 1995.
Omni, Nov. 1993.
"Once Upon a Time, Nike, Wieden & Kennedy and Michael Jordan Weren't Yet a Team." *Advertising Age*, Jan. 25, 1999.
O'Neill, Helen. "Solo Surgery." *Associated Press*, Jan. 3, 1999.
People, Oct. 1991-Aug. 2000.
Peyser, Marc. "Cops and Docs Forever." *Newsweek*, Mar. 27, 2000.
Pogrebin, Robin. "Outside Magazine Succeeds by Defying Categories." *New York Times*, Oct. 27, 1997.
Posnock, Susan Thea. "20 Power Launches for the 90's." *Folio*, Feb. 1, 2000.
Reibstein, Larry. "'Not Guilty' Does Not Mean 'Welcome Back.'" *Newsweek*, Oct. 23, 1995.
Reich, Robert B. "Companies Are Cutting Their Hearts Out." *New York Times,* Dec. 19, 1993.
Rowan, Carl T. "Don't Overlook Powell's Remarkable Life Story." *Chicago Sun-Times*, Oct. 1, 1993.
Rutter, Nancy. "Technology's Wealthiest." *Forbes*, Oct. 5, 1998.
Ryan, James. "She's 18, and Ready or Not, She's a Celebrity." *New York Times*, July 16, 1995.
Schmitt, Eric. "Senators Reject Both Job-Bias Ban and Gay Marriage." *New York Times*, Sept. 11, 1996.
Schonfeld, Erick. "Dress Codes Unravel." *Fortune*, June 27, 1994.
Schoolman, Judith. "Big Stakes in Toy Games." *Daily News*, Feb. 14, 2000.
Schorr, Daniel. "Politics by the Book: Colin Powell." *New Leader*, Oct. 9, 1995.
Schrage, Michael. "Martha Stewart, Interview." *ADWEEK*, Feb. 14, 2000.
Scott, William B. "At 10, Hubble Is National Icon." *Aviation Week & Space Technology*, May 1, 2000.
Slate, Libby. "Young Again." *Los Angeles Times*, June 21, 1992.
Sommers, Susan. "If Such a Look Exists, Calvin Klein, Ralph Lauren, and Donna Karan Are the Ones Who Define It." *Hush*, Vol.1, 1999.
Speer, Tibbet L. "Growing the Green Market." *American Demographics*, Aug. 1997.
Spiegler, Marc. "Marketing Street Culture." *American Demographics*, Nov. 1996.

Sports Illustrated, Apr. 1990-July 2000.
"The State of Garbage in America." *BioCycle*, Apr. 2000.
Stein, Joel. "The Low-Carb Diet Craze." *Health*, Nov. 1, 1999.
Strother, Susan G. "Starbucks is Steaming Into Orlando." *Orlando Sentinel*, Oct. 26, 1998.
Sullivan, Kristina B. "The Latest Telecommuting Gadgets." *PC Week*, Nov. 20, 1995.
"A Sweeping Celebration: The New Century." *Atlanta Journal and Constitution*, Jan. 2, 2000.
Thomas, Karen. "States Take Stab at Regulating Teen Body Piercing." *USA Today*, July 7, 1999.
Time, Apr. 1989-June 2000.
"Turn Left on Main Street." *Newsweek*, Oct. 5, 1998.
Turner, Rob. "This Is Your Future Calling." *Money*, May 2000.
U.S. News & World Report, Jan. 25, 1999.
Very, Jenny P. "Remote Patrol." *Chicago Tribune*, Dec. 22, 1998.
Vincent, Norah. "Confronting the Pride Divide." *Village Voice*, Sept. 7, 1999.
Weiner, Tim. "Selling Weapons: Stealth, Lies and Videotape." *New York Times*, July 14, 1996.
Weinraub, Bernard. "Even on TV, Puberty Can't Last Forever." *New York Times*, May 3, 2000.
Wilke, Michael. "FDA Near Ruling on DTC Drug Ads on TV." *Advertising Age*, June 29, 1998.
Wyly, Michael Duncan. "Combat in the 21st Century." *U.S. News & World Report*, Mar. 16, 1998.

OTHER SOURCES
Avila, Jim. "Americans Buying SUVs in Record Numbers." *NBC News* (TV Transcript), Jan. 6, 2000.
Edwards, Bob. "America's Growing Fascination With Reality Television." *NPR: Morning Edition* (Radio Transcript), Feb. 25, 2000.
Harray, Matt. "'In Contempt' by Christopher Darden." Available: http://www.zoca.com/swallowtail/toolbox/reviews/darden.html N.d.
Hill, Jim. "Kato Kaelin Gives New Details in Simpson Case, Lawyers Say." Available: http://www.cnn.com Feb. 16, 1996.
Hillis, Scott. "Microsoft Break-Up Plan Sparks Shareholder Debate." Available: http://www.yahoo.com Apr. 27, 2000.
"Judge Upholds Simpson Civil Verdict." Available: http://www.lycos.com Apr. 28, 1997.
McGraw, Dan. "Making It: The Long, Hard Road to Fame." Available: http://www.usnews.com May 17, 1999.
Richwine, Lisa. "Microsoft Appeal Could Last a Year." Available: http://www.yahoo.com Apr. 30, 2000.
Ryan, Joal. "'America's Funniest' Denies Saget Out." Available: http://www.eonline.com June 10, 1997.
Siegel, Robert, and Linda Wertheimer. "E-mail Surgery." *NPR: All Things Considered* (Radio Transcript No. 98111806-212), Nov. 18, 1998.
Williams, Juan. "Reality-Based TV." *National Public Radio* (Radio Transcript), Mar. 1, 2000.

WEBSITES CONSULTED
www.abbagirl.com; www.abcnews.go.com; www.about.com; www.adage. com; www.altculture.com; www.amazon.com; www.ask.com; www.britannica.com; www.caranddriver.com; www.cnn.fn.com; www.cs.indiana.edu; www.dailynews.yahoo.com; www.dotcomguy.com; www.ebay.com; www.edmunds.com; www.encarta.msn.com; www.encyclopedia.com; www.espn.go.com/ xgames.html; www.forbes. com; www.ft.com; www.gatesfoundation.org; www.howard.net/ban-suvs.htm; www.imdb.com; www.internet.com; www.investorwords. com; www.ipl.org/ref/POTUS; www.leonardodicaprio.com; www.melroseplacedirect.com; www.metrotimes.com; www.microsoft. com; www2.netdoor.com; www.newt.org; www.nobel.sdsc.edu; www.nytimes.com/library/film; www.oscars.com; www.priceline.com; www.pulitzers.org; www.rockhall.com; www.satellitetech.com; www.SimplyGarth.com; www.snoop-dogg.com; www.suv.org; www.swa.org; www.wchstv.com; www.whitehouse.gov.

INDEX

Numerals in italics indicate an illustration of the subject mentioned.

TIME® LIFE BOOKS

Time-Life Books is a division of Time Life Inc.
Time-Life is a trademark of Time Warner Inc. and affiliated companies.

TIME LIFE INC.
CHAIRMAN AND CHIEF EXECUTIVE OFFICER: Jim Nelson
PRESIDENT AND CHIEF OPERATING OFFICER:
Steven Janas
SENIOR EXECUTIVE VICE PRESIDENT AND
CHIEF OPERATIONS OFFICER: Mary Davis Holt
SENIOR VICE PRESIDENT AND
CHIEF FINANCIAL OFFICER: Christopher Hearing

TIME-LIFE BOOKS
PRESIDENT: Larry Jellen
Senior Vice President, Home and Hearth Markets: Bridget Boel
Vice President, Home and Hearth Markets: Nicholas M. DiMarco
Vice President, Content Development: Jennifer L. Pearce

TIME-LIFE TRADE PUBLISHING
Vice President and Publisher: Neil S. Levin
Senior Sales Director: Richard J. Vreeland
Director, Marketing and Publicity: Inger Forland
Director of Trade Sales: Dana Hobson
Director of Custom Publishing: John Lalor
Director of Rights and Licensing: Olga Vezeris

OUR AMERICAN CENTURY
Marketing Director: Peter Tardif
Senior Editor: Robert Somerville
Director of Design: Tina Taylor
Project Editor: Paula York-Soderlund
Page Makeup Specialist: Jennifer Gearhart
Production Manager: Virginia Reardon
Quality Assurance: Jim King and Stacy L. Eddy

Design for Our American Century by Antonio Alcalá, Studio A, Alexandria, Virginia
The Digital Decade: The 90s produced by Bishop Books, New York, New York

Special Contributors
Celia Beattie, Esther Ferington, Louise Forstall, Mary Beth Oelkers-Keegan, Alan Pitts

10 9 8 7 6 5 4 3 2 1

Library of Congress Cataloging-in-Publication Data
The digital decade—the 90s / by the editors of Time-Life Books.
   p. cm—(Our American century)
  Includes bibliographical references and index.
  ISBN 0-7835-5521-0
  1. United States—History—1969– 2. Nineteen nineties. 3. United States—History—1969– Pictorial works. 4. Nineteen nineties—Pictorial works. I. Time-Life Books. II. Series.

E881 .D54 2000
973.929—dc21   00-060747

EDITORIAL CONSULTANT
Richard B. Stolley is currently senior editorial adviser at Time Inc. After 19 years at *Life* magazine as a reporter, bureau chief, and assistant managing editor, he became the first managing editor of *People* magazine, a position he held with great success for eight years. He then returned to *Life* magazine as managing editor and later served as editorial director for all Time Inc. magazines. In 1997 Stolley received the Henry Johnson Fisher Award for Lifetime Achievement, the magazine industry's highest honor.

Other History Publications:
World War II
What Life Was Like
The American Story
Voices of the Civil War
The American Indians

For information on and a full description of any of the Time-Life Books series listed above, please call 1-800-621-7026 or write:
Reader Information
Time-Life Customer Service
P.O. Box C-32068
Richmond, Virginia 23261-2068

On the cover: At the Washington Monument in Washington, D.C., fireworks celebrating the new millennium were part of a three-hour extravaganza. At some cities around the world, preparations for the global bash took as long as three years. Pictured from left to right at the top of the cover are some of the decade's notable figures: President Bill Clinton, actress Julia Roberts, magazine publisher John F. Kennedy Jr., Secretary of State Madeleine K. Albright, television talk-show host Rosie O'Donnell, and basketball great Michael Jordan. On the spine is Bill Gates, chairman and CEO of Microsoft.